SQL for Beginners: Building Strong Database Foundations

Your Essential Guide to Querying and Managing Databases

Emily Harris

Table of Contents

INTRODUCTION

Welcome to the book "SQL for Beginners: Building Strong Database Foundations: Your Essential Guide to Querying and Managing Databases." This book is your key to unlocking the power of SQL (Structured Query Language), the universal language for interacting with relational databases. Whether you're a novice programmer, an ambitious data analyst, or someone who wants to enhance their technical abilities, this guide will equip you with the fundamental understanding and useful abilities to efficiently query and manage databases, empowering you to take control of your data.

Database administration is a crucial skill in today's data-driven environment. Databases form the backbone of various applications, from simple web pages to complex enterprise systems. Mastering SQL will not only help you organize, retrieve, and work with data effectively, but also make you a valuable asset in the job market. This book ensures that you have a solid understanding of database foundations by breaking down complex topics into manageable, practical chunks.

You will learn to configure your system, comprehend database schemas, compose simple and complex SQL queries, work with data, and guarantee data security. Every chapter has several exercises, real-world examples, and helpful hints to help you learn and gain confidence.

By the end of this book, you will be well-equipped to handle SQL databases, laying a solid basis for your future data-related activities. Greetings on your path to learning SQL!

CHAPTER I

Say Hello To Databases and SQL

What is a Database?

An electronically stored and accessible collection of well-organized data is called a database. A database's primary function is to offer an organized setting for effectively managing, retrieving, and storing data. Modern computing is only possible with databases, which are the foundation of countless applications ranging from straightforward inventory tracking systems to intricate financial systems and expansive Internet services.

Fundamentally, a database is made to address data management issues, namely data integrity, redundancy, and inconsistency. A database ensures that several people may access and modify data in an organized and regulated way by centralizing it in one place. Additionally, data integrity is ensured by facilitating centralization, guaranteeing that information is dependable, accurate, and consistent over time. Databases also offer data security features, guaranteeing that private data is shielded from unwanted access.

Relational and non-relational databases are the primary categories into which databases may be roughly divided. Every sort has advantages and works well for various applications and data management requirements.

Data is arranged into tables in relational databases, commonly called SQL databases. Every table has rows and columns, where a row denotes a single record, and a column is a field contained in the record. Tables are one way to depict the concept of relations, which is the foundation of the relational model. Relational databases are powerful because they manage and manipulate data using Structured Query Language (SQL). Users may carry out various tasks with SQL, a standardized language, such as maintaining database structures, updating records, and querying data.

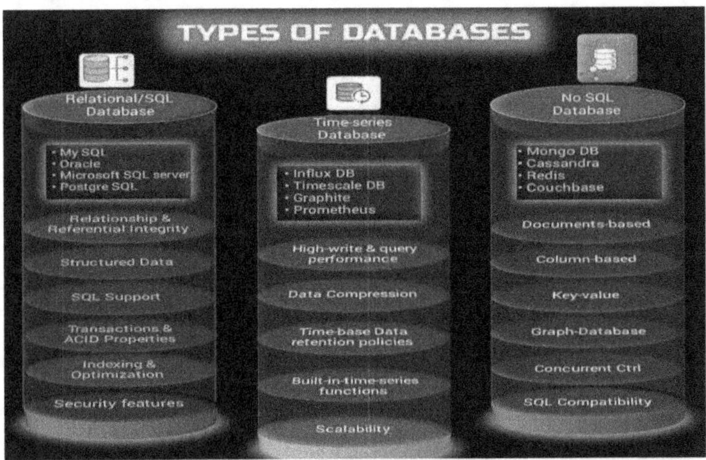

Relational databases' primary benefit is their capacity to manage structured data with intricate relationships. Foreign keys are used to create associations between distinct tables, whereas primary keys are used to identify records within a table uniquely. Users can now link tables and get data based on intricate criteria thanks to the robust querying capabilities made possible by this. Relational databases also provide transactions, guaranteeing that a sequence of events either successfully culminate as a group or are entirely reversed, preserving the data's integrity.

Relational databases with a broad appeal include MySQL, PostgreSQL, Oracle Database, and Microsoft SQL Server. These databases are widely used in many sectors, including e-commerce, education, healthcare, and finance. To maintain accuracy and consistency across all records, a banking system, for example, can utilize a relational database to store customer accounts, transactions, and other financial data.

Non-relational databases, or NoSQL databases, provide another method for managing data. They do not arrange data into tables, in contrast to relational databases. Instead, they employ a variety of data models, including graph, document, key-value, and column-family databases. NoSQL databases can manage unstructured and semi-structured data more effectively because of this flexibility.

JSON-like documents are used as data storage in document databases like CouchDB and MongoDB. A document's structure can vary from document to document, giving data representation more freedom. Because of this, document databases are ideal for applications like content management systems and real-time analytics that need a dynamic schema.

Key-value pairs are used by key-value databases like Redis and DynamoDB to store data. This straightforward and effective architecture is perfect for applications like caching and session management that demand quick read-and-write operations. With minimal latency, the key-value approach can process massive amounts of data and is very scalable.

Instead of storing data in rows, column-family databases like Apache Cassandra and HBase store it in columns. This architecture is intended to manage massive amounts of data among dispersed systems. Large datasets can be stored and retrieved quickly in column-family databases frequently utilized in big data applications.

Nodes and edges represent entities and their relationships and store data in graph databases like Neo4j and Amazon Neptune. Applications involving complex relationships, such as social networks, recommendation engines, and fraud detection systems, benefit greatly from this paradigm. Relationship-centric applications benefit significantly from graph databases' speedy traversal and querying of connected data.

There are a wide variety of real-world instances of database use cases. Relational databases are utilized in the healthcare sector to store patient data, appointments, and billing details. These systems enhance operational effectiveness and treatment quality by guaranteeing that patient data is correct and available to authorized medical staff. On the other hand, non-relational databases are used to evaluate vast amounts of medical data, including sensor data from wearable devices and genomic sequences, enabling tailored care and advanced research.

Platforms for e-commerce also rely significantly on databases. Inventory levels, customer orders, and product catalogs are all managed using relational databases. Customers may track orders, manage their accounts, and search for products using these databases' sophisticated queries. However, recommendation engines and personalization features run on non-relational databases, which examine user behavior and preferences to offer customized product recommendations.

Social media networks combine relational and non-relational databases to manage their enormous volumes of data. Relational databases preserve the consistency and integrity of data by managing user accounts, friendships, and message history. Non-relational databases store and analyze unstructured data for real-time feed updates and content recommendations, including multimedia material, postings, and comments.

Relational databases are necessary in the finance industry to manage accounts, transactions, and financial instruments. These databases enhance regulatory compliance and risk management by guaranteeing the accuracy and consistency of economic data. Using real-time analysis of massive amounts of transaction data, non-relational databases are utilized to spot patterns and abnormalities that point to possible fraud.

Databases are used in many other fields as well. For example, they are used in education to manage student records, course catalogs, and academic performance data; in telecommunications to handle call logs, customer information, and network configurations; and in logistics to manage warehouse inventories, track shipments, and optimize supply chain operations.

In summary, databases are essential tools for managing and organizing data in today's society. They offer an organized setting that guarantees data protection, efficiency, and integrity. Non-relational databases provide flexibility and scalability for unstructured and semi-structured data, while relational databases are best at managing structured data with intricate relationships. Relational or non-relational databases may be selected depending on the particular needs of the application and the type of data being maintained. Databases are essential for promoting efficiency and innovation in various industries due to their broad uses

Introduction to SQL

Structured Query Language, or SQL, is a popular and potent programming language for handling relational databases. Working with databases requires understanding SQL since it allows for a wide range of actions, from building and managing database structures to querying data. This section explores the meaning and background of SQL, its significance in database administration, an outline of SQL standards, and how to set up a SQL environment.

Early in the 1970s, Donald D. Chamberlin and Raymond F. Boyce invented SQL at IBM. Due to trademark concerns, the original name, Structured English Query Language, or SEQUEL, was eventually changed to SQL. Based on the relational paradigm put forth by Edgar F.

Codd, the language was created to be a domain-specific language for managing data stored in a relational database management system (RDBMS). Data are arranged into tables, or relations, according to the relational model, and these tables can be connected based on shared data. With the help of SQL, users may interact with these tables in a standardized manner and carry out several tasks, including controlling the data and its structure and searching and changing it.

One cannot stress the importance of SQL in database management. It is the primary language RDBMSs use, the foundation of most contemporary applications that need dependable, effective data retrieval and storage. SQL allows users to design, manipulate, and enforce data integrity restrictions on their data. It makes sophisticated querying features necessary for data analysis and reporting possible, including the ability to filter, sort, and aggregate data. Additionally, SQL allows for transactional operations, essential for preserving data integrity in multi-user contexts by enabling the reliable and consistent execution of numerous database changes.

The fact that SQL is used by many different database systems, including open-source MySQL and PostgreSQL and popular commercial systems like Oracle, Microsoft SQL Server, and IBM Db2, further emphasizes the significance of SQL. Because of its broad use, SQL is now a necessary competency for many IT professionals, including database administrators, developers, and data analysts. Writing effective SQL queries is crucial to maximizing database performance and guaranteeing the seamless operation of applications.

Over time, several SQL standards have been created to aid with standardization and interoperability. Several SQL standards have been issued by the International Organization for Standardization (ISO) and the American National Standards Institute (ANSI). The SQL-86 standard was the first, and further standards include SQL-89, SQL-92, SQL:1999, SQL:2003, SQL:2006, SQL:2008, SQL:2011, SQL:2016, and SQL:2019. New features and improvements have been added to the standard with each iteration, including object-oriented features, procedural extensions, support for XML, and enhanced concurrency control techniques. Although these standards aim to guarantee interoperability amongst various SQL implementations, each database system has its own unique extensions and modifications in practice. While sophisticated features and optimizations may vary, basic SQL syntax and operations remain the same.

The first natural step to learning SQL is setting up your SQL environment. Choosing a database management system (DBMS), setting it up for use, and installing the required software are the steps in the process. Several factors, such as your particular use case, performance needs, and system familiarity, will determine which database management system (DBMS) is best for you. MySQL and PostgreSQL are well-liked options for novices because of their comprehensive documentation, vibrant communities, and simplicity of use.

Installing the software is the next step after selecting a DBMS. This uses the MySQL Installer, which can be downloaded from the official website and installed by following the installation instructions. A similar procedure can be used to install PostgreSQL by downloading the installer from the PostgreSQL website. You can choose from default settings or tailor the installation to your requirements, as both installers will walk you through the installation procedure.

You must configure a client tool after installing the DBMS to communicate with the database. With MySQL, pgAdmin is a commonly used graphical user interface (GUI) application, whereas MySQL Workbench is popular with PostgreSQL. These tools offer an easy-to-use interface for managing database objects, running SQL queries, and handling administrative duties. Alternatively, you can take advantage of the more direct control over database operations offered by the DBMS's command-line tools, like the MySQL command-line client or psql for PostgreSQL.

Creating initial database schemas, defining access rights, and configuring users are all part of database configuration. This is a critical step in ensuring your data is organized and secure. SQL statements like CREATE USER and GRANT allow you to create a new user in MySQL and grant them rights. Similarly, PostgreSQL lets you use SQL commands to handle users and roles. You can design your database schema by specifying tables, columns, data types, and relationships after users and permissions have been set up.

Making a database connection is the last step in configuring your environment. Using a command-line client or a graphical user interface tool, you must supply connection information, such as the hostname, port number, database name, and user credentials. After connecting, you may begin interacting with your database by running SQL queries. To become comfortable with the syntax, starting with basic questions and working your way up to more complicated operations as you develop confidence is best.

SQL provides a standardized interface for interacting with and manipulating data, making it an essential tool for relational database management. Since its inception in the early days of database technology, it has become a crucial ability for IT professionals working in various fields. To fully utilize SQL in your applications, you must first set up a suitable SQL environment. Understanding SQL standards guarantees compatibility and efficiency. Whatever your career goals—developer, data analyst, or database administrator—learning SQL will teach you the skills to administer and access databases successfully.

Setting Up Your Environment

One of the most critical steps in learning database management and manipulation is setting up your SQL environment. Choosing the appropriate programming tools, installing an SQL database, and completing essential connection and configuration chores are all part of the process. This section will walk you through these processes using examples from two of the most widely used SQL databases, PostgreSQL and MySQL, and the related development tools, pgAdmin and MySQL Workbench.

Selecting an SQL database management system is the initial stage in configuring your SQL environment (DBMS). For novices and experts alike, MySQL and PostgreSQL are great options because of their dependability, robust feature sets, and large communities of users. The Oracle Corporation's MySQL is a popular online application database well-known for its strong performance and ease of use. An open-source DBMS called PostgreSQL is famous for its sophisticated capabilities and adherence to SQL standards, which makes it a top choice for intricate applications and extensive installations.

First, download the MySQL Installer from the official MySQL website to install MySQL. The installer provides a handy setup wizard that walks you through the installation procedure. A standard installation comes with the MySQL server, MySQL Workbench, and other necessary parts; alternatively, you can opt for a bespoke installation in which you can choose which parts to install. The MySQL server needs to be set up after installation. Using the setup wizard, you can configure network settings (including port number), authentication techniques, and the kind of server (development, server machine, or dedicated machine). After configuring these parameters, you establish a root account with a strong password and optionally add other users.

The procedure for installing PostgreSQL is similar. The PostgreSQL website offers the installer for download. You can select the installation path and the components to install, including the graphical user interface tool pgAdmin, as the installation wizard walks you through the setup process. Installing PostgreSQL requires you to configure the port number for the server and establish a password for the default PostgreSQL superuser, 'Postgres.' After the installation is finished, the PostgreSQL server will launch immediately. You may then access your database using the command-line interface or pgAdmin.

The next step is to choose your SQL development tools after installing your SQL database. For MySQL and PostgreSQL, two well-liked options are MySQl Workbench and pgAdmin. These tools offer graphical user interfaces that make database management, SQL query creation and execution, and administrative chores easier.

A unified visual tool for database architects, developers, and DBAs is MySQL Workbench. It provides SQL creation, data modeling, and extensive management features. You can create, modify, and execute SQL queries with the SQL Editor function and manage and design your database schemas using the visual data modeling feature. Tools for database migration, server configuration, user management, backup, and recovery are also included in MySQL Workbench. Because of its simple and user-friendly layout, even novice users may easily navigate it and access complex functions for more seasoned users.

However, the most widely used open-source PostgreSQL administration and development platform is PgAdmin. Running SQL queries and managing PostgreSQL databases is simple with its user-friendly interface. A graphical query builder, a SQL editor with syntax highlighting, and tools for tracking server performance and activity are some of the features offered by PgAdmin. Additionally, it provides sophisticated features, including extensive reporting capabilities and procedural language debugging. Like MySQL Workbench, pgAdmin is made to be as strong as it is intuitive, making it suitable for a broad spectrum of users, from beginners to experienced database administrators.

Following installing your SQL database and selecting your programming tools, the following stage involves basic setup and connectivity. This entails connecting from your programming tool, configuring your database server, and creating users and databases.

For MySQL, you can use MySQL Workbench to manage your server configuration after finishing the initial setup with the MySQL Installer. You may monitor server performance, manage user accounts, and modify server settings with MySQL Workbench's "Server Administration" tool. You can use the SQL Editor to run the "CREATE DATABASE" command to create a new database. A new database called "my database" will be created; for instance, if you run "CREATE DATABASE my database," The "CREATE TABLE" command can then build tables inside this database, specifying the required columns and data types.

It's simple to connect to your MySQL database with MySQL Workbench. Launch MySQL Workbench, then select "New Connection" from the menu. Enter the connection name, hostname (often 'localhost' for local installations), port number (by default 3306), username (e.g., 'root'), and password in the "Set up a New Connection" window. Click "Test Connection" to confirm the connection after providing these details. You can access your MySQL server and databases by saving the connection if it works.

With PostgreSQL, you may control your server configuration and database objects using pgAdmin once the installation and basic setup are finished. Performance data and server activities are displayed on a dashboard that PgAdmin offers. In the object browser, right-click on the "Databases" node and choose "Create" -> "Database" to start a new database. Enter the database name and owner (often the 'Postgres' user) in the "Create Database" window, then click "Save". Then, you can use the graphical user interface or the query editor's SQL commands to construct tables in this database.

A new server connection is necessary when using pgAdmin to connect to your PostgreSQL database. Click on the "Add New Server" option after opening pgAdmin. Enter the connection information in the "Create - Server" window, which should contain the server name, hostname (such as "localhost"), port number (by default, 5432), maintenance database (often "Postgres"), username (such as "Postgres"), and password. To establish the connection, click "Save" once you've entered these details. Once connected, you can explore your databases, run SQL queries, and perform other administrative functions with pgAdmin.

To sum up, a few essential processes are involved in setting up your SQL environment: picking and installing an SQL database, selecting suitable development tools, and completing connection and configuration tasks. PostgreSQL and MySQL are great options for SQL databases because they have a sizeable community-supporting base and strong feature sets. Robust programs that offer intuitive interfaces for database management and SQL query execution are MySQL Workbench and pgAdmin. You may successfully set up your SQL environment and start using SQL's power to manage and alter your data by following the instructions provided in this section. An adequately designed SQL environment is necessary for effective and efficient database management, regardless of experience level.

CHAPTER II

Understanding Database Concepts

Database Schema

A database schema is the architecture or blueprint for how data is arranged inside a database. It establishes the kinds, structures, and connections between data, offering a well-defined structure for effectively storing and retrieving information. Designing reliable and efficient databases requires understanding the elements of a database schema, including tables, columns, rows, data types, constraints, and keys.

The essential components of a relational database schema are tables. Each table comprises rows and columns and represents an entity, such as customers, orders, or items. What kind of data can be stored in a table is determined by its structure. For example, columns for customer ID, name, address, phone number, and email address can be in a "Customers" database. A single record or instance of the entity, such as a particular client, is represented by each row in this table.

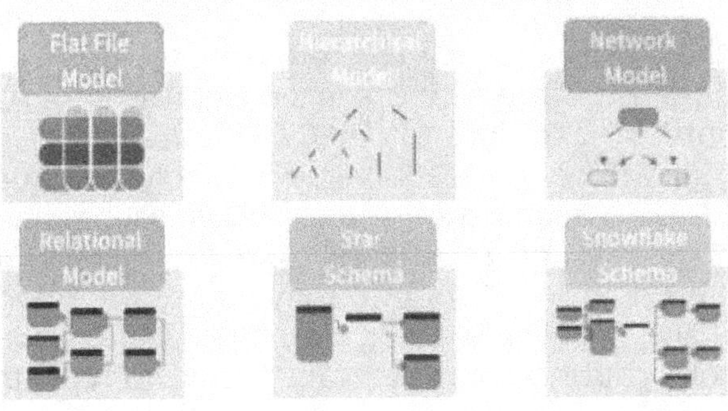

A table's columns specify which specific data fields it can contain. The data type that can be stored in each column is determined by its type: an integer, varchar (variable character), date, or boolean. Constraints on columns can also impose guidelines on the data. For instance, a "NOT NULL" constraint guarantees that a column must include data in each row and cannot have a null value. Within the database, constraints support the preservation of data consistency and integrity.

The horizontal items in a table are called rows, sometimes referred to as records or tuples. A distinct collection of data fields that match the columns are present in each row. For instance, a single entry in a "Customers" table might contain data about a single customer, including their ID, name, address, phone number, and email. The data entries that make up a table are called rows, and SQL procedures can add, edit, or remove them.

Data types are essential to define the data that is kept in each column. Common data types include dates for date and time values, booleans for actual/false values, varchars for strings or text, and integers for numerical data. The type of data that is chosen has an impact on how it is processed and stored. For instance, using an integer data type rather than a varchar type is more efficient when performing numerical computations. A proper definition of data types guarantees adequate data storage and accurate manipulation and retrieval.

Rules that are applied to columns to ensure data consistency and integrity are called constraints. Typical constraints in addition to "NOT NULL" are "UNIQUE," which guarantees that each value in a column is unique, and "CHECK," which establishes a requirement that each value in the column must meet. For example, a CHECK constraint on an "Age" column may be used to guarantee that the age is a positive number. If no value is supplied for a column during data insertion, "DEFAULT" constraints offer a default value. These limitations are essential for guaranteeing that the data complies with the established guidelines and avoiding erroneous data from entering the database.

A primary key is one constraint that gives each row in a table a unique identity. A central key cannot have null values and must have exceptional values. Primary keys, like an order number or customer ID, are typically defined on a single column. However, they can also comprise numerous columns, a composite primary key. Primary keys are necessary to index and retrieve data quickly to guarantee that every record can be identified and returned individually. They enable reliable data management and retrieval and are fundamental to relational database architecture.

Another crucial component of database schema design is foreign keys. A column, or group of columns, in one table that refers to the primary key in another table is called a foreign key. This connects the two tables by using their shared key to bind them together. A foreign key column named "CustomerID" in the "Orders" database, for instance, might relate to the "CustomerID" primary key in the "Customers" table. Foreign keys uphold referential integrity by guaranteeing that the value in the foreign key column corresponds to a legitimate primary key value in the associated table. This relationship is necessary to enable complicated searches that integrate data from various tables and guarantee consistency across tables.

Relational database architecture is based on the interaction between primary and foreign keys, which enables the construction of normalized databases with the most minor dependencies and redundancies. Normalization entails arranging data into tables and establishing linkages to minimize data duplication and enhance data integrity. Usually, this procedure adheres to a set of guidelines, standard forms, that direct the schema's design to guarantee effective data organization.

Each table in a well-designed database architecture concentrates on a particular entity, with the primary keys guaranteeing records are uniquely identified and the columns expressing the entity's qualities. Foreign keys create relationships between tables by tying together relevant data and ensuring referential integrity. A normalized database for an e-commerce application, for instance, would have tables labeled "Products," "Orders," "Customers," and "OrderDetails." A foreign key connecting the "Orders" table to the "Customers" table and a foreign key connecting the "OrderDetails" table to the "Orders" and "Products" tables would be present. This structure makes efficient data retrieval and manipulation possible, opening the door to sophisticated searches that integrate data from several tables.

Beyond these basic ideas, sophisticated features and factors can improve a database schema's resilience and efficiency even more. Creating an index on one or more columns is indexing, which helps speed up data retrieval. Indexing greatly benefits columns that are regularly utilized in joint operations or search conditions. They can, however, also affect the speed of data insertion, update, and deletion activities and necessitate more storage space. Therefore, special consideration must be given when creating indexes to balance query performance and maintenance overhead.

Utilizing views, virtual tables made by querying data from one or more underlying tables is another crucial component. Views can improve security by limiting access to particular data, streamlining complicated queries, and offering a standardized user interface across several apps. Materialized views can increase performance for frequently requested data by physically storing the query result; however, they also come with additional storage and maintenance requirements.

In addition, triggers and stored procedures are crucial components of database schema design. Precompiled SQL statements, known as stored procedures, allow complex processes to be carried out efficiently and consistently as a single entity. Triggers are unique stored procedures running automatically when specific things happen, such as adding, updating, or deleting data. They help with task automation inside the database, audit trail maintenance, and business rule enforcement.

In summary, efficient data administration and manipulation depend on a well-designed database schema. It entails putting data into tables, specifying columns with the correct data and limitations, and using primary and foreign keys to create relationships between them. By adhering to recommended techniques for schema design, including indexing, normalization, and utilizing views, stored procedures, and triggers, you can build a dependable database that facilitates data retrieval, storage, and analysis. Anybody working with relational databases has to understand these ideas since they are the cornerstone of developing high-performance, scalable, and maintainable database systems.

Normalization and Data Integrity

In database architecture, normalization and data integrity are essential ideas that guarantee effective data organization, minimize duplication, and preserve data quality and consistency. Normalization is arranging a relational database's fields and tables to reduce dependencies and redundancies. Standard forms are a set of norms or rules that serve as a guide for this process. In contrast, data integrity pertains to preserving the precision and coherence of data during its entire existence. A key component of database performance and integrity is indexes, which facilitate quicker record retrieval and guarantee effective query execution.

The First Normal Form (1NF) is the first step toward normalization. If all of the values in a table are atomic (indivisible) and only one type of value appears in each column, the table is said to be in 1NF. This signifies that a single piece of data, not a collection or list of values, should be stored in each table cell. For example, if a table in a student database has a phone number column, then each cell in that column should have a single phone number. This guarantees that the data is correctly arranged into rows and columns and eliminates repetitive groups.

The requirements of 1NF are expanded upon in the Second Normal Form (2NF). If a table is in 1NF and every non-key attribute depends entirely on the primary key for functionality, then the table is in 2NF. Every non-key attribute should be connected to the primary key, not just a subset. Every non-key column in a composite critical scenario—where the primary key comprises several columns—must rely on every primary key component. This eliminates partial dependency, which can cause anomalies in the insertion, update, and deletion of data and redundancy. An employee-project combination, for instance, should be uniquely identified by each row in an employee project assignment table, and non-key variables like hours worked should depend on both the project ID and the employee ID.

A further step is taken by the Third Normal Form (3NF), which does away with transitive reliance. If a table is in 2NF and its characteristics depend only on the primary key for functionality, it is in 3NF. It follows that non-key qualities shouldn't be dependent on one another. For instance, in a table containing department and employee data, the department name should be determined by the department ID, which serves as the primary key for the department table rather than the employee ID. We guarantee that every information is kept in a single location by organizing data into 3NF, which lowers redundancy and enhances data integrity.

The Boyce-Codd Normal Form (BCNF), Fourth Normal Form (4NF), and Fifth Normal Form (5NF) are higher standard forms that go beyond 3NF. A more robust variant of 3NF, BCNF, addresses some abnormalities that 3NF does not cover. If a table is in 3NF and X is a superkey for any non-trivial functional dependency X -> Y, then the table is in BCNF. This implies that a superkey should be the determinant for every dependency. To handle multi-valued dependencies, 4NF ensures that there shouldn't be more than one independent multi-valued attribute for every primary key value. To prevent a table from being divided into smaller tables without losing data, 5NF handles join dependencies.

Data integrity requires several crucial procedures and systems. Utilizing constraints like primary keys, foreign keys, unique constraints, and check constraints is essential. Duplicate records are avoided using primary keys, guaranteeing each is individually recognizable. Foreign keys preserve referential integrity by ensuring that a value in one table matches a legitimate value in another. While check constraints impose particular requirements that every value in a column must meet, unique constraints guarantee that values in a column or a set of columns remain unique across the table.

Indexes are essential for both performance optimization and data integrity. A data structure called an index helps database tables retrieve data more quickly. Columns that are often utilized in join operations or search conditions are index-created. For instance, queries that look for orders by customer ID might be sped up considerably by indexing the customer ID field in an orders table. Indexes might be unique or non-unique, single-column or multi-column (composite indexes). Data integrity is enforced by unique indexes, which make sure that no two entries in the indexed column have the same value.

It is impossible to overestimate the significance of indexes since they improve database performance and enable adequate data access. A database management system (DBMS) would have to search the whole table without indexes to locate the pertinent rows, which can be extremely time-consuming, particularly for large tables. Indexes facilitate rapid lookups by offering an organized path to the data, which minimizes the time and resources needed for query execution. On the other hand, indexes also have maintenance and storage costs. Every time there is a modification to the data in the indexed columns, they must be updated, which may affect how quickly insert, update, and delete actions are completed.

It is crucial to select the appropriate columns for indexing to weigh the advantages and disadvantages of the process. Primary keys and foreign keys are usually indexed by default. Indexing should also consider columns often utilized in join operations, sorting, and search conditions. It is not recommended, however, to index every column as this can result in high maintenance costs and decreased write performance. Database managers must closely examine query patterns and performance indicators to identify the most valuable indexes.

Apart from indexes, triggers, and stored procedures are additional strategies that can aid in preserving data integrity. Triggers are unique stored procedures running automatically in reaction to particular table events like insertions, updates, or deletions. They can be applied to uphold accurate and consistent data, audit modifications, and enforce business rules. For instance, a trigger can automatically update a product's table's stock quantity each time a new order is placed.

Precompiled SQL statements that can be run simultaneously are called stored procedures. They offer a means of enforcing data integrity regulations and encapsulating intricate business logic. For instance, a stored method can guarantee that the customer's credit limit won't be surpassed when a new order is placed. We may guarantee consistent enforcement of data integrity standards across many apps and user interfaces by centralizing business logic into stored procedures.

To sum up, data integrity and normalization are essential elements of a successful database architecture. Normalization minimizes duplication and reliance by classifying information into tables and defining relationships per standard standards. Constraints, indexes, triggers, and stored procedures are tools used to maintain data quality and consistency. Specifically, indexes are essential for preserving data integrity and maximizing database efficiency. Database designers and administrators can build scalable, dependable, and effective databases that enable robust data management and retrieval by comprehending and implementing these principles.

Entity-Relationship Model

The Entity-Relationship (ER) model is a foundational concept in database design, enabling data representation in a structured and systematic way. The ER model developed by Peter Chen in 1976 provides a visual framework to illustrate the relationships between data entities within a system. This model uses ER diagrams to graphically depict entities, their attributes, and the relationships among them, thereby facilitating a clear understanding of data interconnections and dependencies.

At the heart of the ER model are entities, which represent objects or concepts that can be distinctly identified within a database. Each entity is characterized by a set of attributes that define its properties. For example, in a university database, entities might include Students, Courses, and Professors, each with characteristics such as Student_ID, Course_Name, and Professor_ID, respectively. These attributes provide detailed information about each entity and are crucial for identifying and distinguishing individual instances of the entities.

Relationships in an ER diagram illustrate how entities are related to one another. These relationships are categorized into three primary types: one-to-one, one-to-many, and many-to-many. Understanding these relationships is essential for accurate database design and ensuring data integrity.

A one-to-one relationship occurs when a single instance of one entity is associated with a single instance of another entity. For example, consider a scenario where each student in a university is assigned a unique student ID card. In this case, a one-to-one relationship exists between the Student entity and the ID_Card entity. Each student possesses exactly one ID card, and each is assigned to precisely one student. One-to-one relationships are relatively rare in database design but valuable in specific situations requiring unique pairings.

A one-to-many relationship is more common and occurs when a single instance of one entity is associated with multiple instances of another entity. For example, in a university database, a professor can teach various courses, but only one professor teaches each course. This creates a one-to-many relationship between the Professor entity and the Course entity. One-to-many relationships are crucial for capturing hierarchical structures and dependencies within data.

Many-to-many relationships are even more prevalent and occur when multiple instances of one entity are associated with various instances of another. An example of this is the relationship between students and courses in a university. A student can enroll in multiple classes, each with multiple students enrolled. This creates a many-to-many relationship between the Student entity and the Course entity. An associative entity called a junction table or a bridge table, effectively represents relationships in a relational database. This table typically contains foreign keys that reference the primary keys of the two related entities, thus resolving the many-to-many relationship into two one-to-many relationships.

Mapping ER models to SQL schemas involves translating the conceptual representation of data into a physical database schema that can be implemented in a relational database management system (RDBMS). This process begins with identifying the entities and their attributes and then defining the primary keys for each entity. Primary keys are unique identifiers that ensure each instance of an entity is distinct.

For example, consider the entities Student, Course, and Professor. The Student entity might have attributes such as Student_ID (primary key), Name, and Major. The Course entity could have Course_ID (primary key), Course_Name, and Credits, while the Professor entity might include Professor_ID (primary key), Name, and Department. Once the entities and their attributes are defined, their relationships are mapped.

In a one-to-one relationship, a foreign key is added to one of the tables to reference the primary key of the other table. For instance, if each student has a unique ID card, the Student table might include an ID_Card_ID attribute that references the primary key of the ID_Card table.

A foreign key in a one-to-many relationship is added to the table on the "many" side. For example, in the one-to-many relationship between professors and courses, the Course table would include a Professor_ID attribute that references the primary key of the Professor table. This ensures that each course is linked to a single professor.

For many-to-many relationships, an associative entity or junction table is created. In the example of students and courses, a Student_Course table would be made with at least two attributes: Student_ID and Course_ID. These attributes would serve as foreign keys referencing the primary keys of the Student and Course tables, respectively. This junction table allows multiple students to be associated with various courses and vice versa.

Once the entities, attributes, primary keys, and foreign keys are defined, SQL statements can be written to create the corresponding tables in the database. The CREATE TABLE statement is used for this purpose. For example, the SQL schema for the Student, Course, and Professor entities might look like this:

s" CREATE TABLE Student (Student_ID INT PRIMARY KEY, Name VARCHAR(100), Major VARCHAR(100));

CREATE TABLE Course (Course_ID INT PRIMARY KEY, Course_Name VARCHAR(100), Credits INT, Professor_ID INT,

FOREIGN KEY (Professor_ID) REFERENCES Professor(Professor_ID)); CREATE TABLE Professor (Professor_ID INT PRIMARY KEY, Name VARCHAR(100), Department VARCHAR(100)).

CREATE TABLE Student_Course (Student_ID INT, Course_ID INT, PRIMARY KEY (Student_ID, Course_ID),

FOREIGN KEY (Student_ID) REFERENCES Student(Student_ID), FOREIGN KEY (Course_ID) REFERENCES Course(Course_ID)).

In this schema, the Student_Course table is the junction table to manage the many-to-many relationship between students and courses. This approach ensures the database structure is normalized, reducing redundancy and improving data integrity.

In summary, the Entity-Relationship model is a vital tool in database design, providing a clear and organized way to represent data and its interrelationships. ER diagrams visually depict entities, attributes, and relationships, which can then be mapped to SQL schemas for implementation in a relational database. Understanding and correctly applying one-to-one, one-to-many, and many-to-many relationships are crucial for creating efficient and reliable databases. This process ensures data is accurately represented and easily accessible, facilitating better management and utilization.

CHAPTER III

Basic SQL Queries

Introduction to SQL Syntax

Structured Query Language (SQL) is not just a common language for communicating with relational databases, it's a powerful tool that empowers users to add, edit, remove, and create data. Its widespread use is a testament to its robust features and user-friendly syntax, which enable effective data management and modification. For anyone working with databases, understanding the fundamental structure of SQL statements, particularly the SELECT, FROM, and WHERE clauses, is a key to unlocking this power.

The SELECT statement, a fundamental SQL statement, is a versatile tool for retrieving data from one or more tables. Composed of the SELECT clause, the FROM clause, and the optional WHERE clause, it forms the backbone of SQL queries. Each clause serves a distinct purpose, providing a potent tool for data retrieval. Mastering these clauses will give you the confidence to handle even the most complex data retrieval and manipulation tasks.

The desired columns of data to be retrieved are specified in the SELECT clause. One or more table columns may be used in this. For instance, you would type {SELECT name, email FROM users;` to choose the users' names and email addresses from a user's table. To pick every column from a table, the asterisk (*) can also be used as a wildcard in the pick clause: `SELECT * FROM users;.` This is quite helpful when you require all the data without having to define each column separately.

Furthermore, SQL allows you to use the AS keyword to rename columns in the result set. This can help to meet specific output requirements and improve readability. To change the results' columns to user_name and user_email, respectively, type {SELECT name AS user_name, email AS user_email FROM users;}.

The table or tables from which the data should be retrieved are specified in the FROM clause. It consists of just one table in its most basic form: `SELECT * FROM users;}. On the other hand, SQL enables more intricate queries that use several tables and JOIN operations to integrate relevant data. There are various JOIN kinds, each with a distinct function, including FULL OUTER JOIN, LEFT JOIN, RIGHT JOIN, and INNER JOIN. A LEFT JOIN, on the other hand, obtains all rows from the left table and the matching rows from the right table, filling in NULLs for non-matching rows. For instance, an INNER JOIN retrieves only the rows with matching values in both tables. `SELECT users.name, orders.order_date FROM users INNER JOIN orders ON users.id = orders.user_id;` illustrates a JOIN operation. By matching the user IDs in both tables, this query obtains the names of users and the order dates that belong to them.

You can only receive data that satisfies specific criteria by filtering entries based on predetermined requirements by using the WHERE clause. Including conditional expressions accomplishes this. To extract all users over 30, use `SELECT * FROM users WHERE age > 30;`. Many operators for comparisons, including {=}, {<>} (not equal), {>}, {<}, {>=}, and `<=}, are supported by the WHERE clause. It can also combine numerous conditions using logical operators like AND, OR, and NOT. To find individuals who are over 30 and reside in New York, for example, run `SELECT * FROM users WHERE age > 30 AND city = 'New York';.` The WHERE clause can additionally use pattern matching with the LIKE operator and wildcard characters to look for particular patterns in string data. The query `SELECT * FROM users WHERE name LIKE 'J%';,` for instance, returns people whose names begin with the letter 'J.' Furthermore, as in `SELECT * FROM users WHERE city IN ('New York,' 'Los Angeles,' 'Chicago'),` the IN operator can indicate many alternative values for a column.

These clauses can be combined to create extremely accurate and personalized queries. Consider, for example, a database with two tables: users and orders, each of which has a link to a user. You may use a query similar to this one to locate people who have placed orders during the last month: `SELECT users—name, orders.order_date FROM users INNER JOIN orders ON users. Where orders.order_date > '2023-05-01';}.id = orders.user_id. For orders placed after May 1, 2023, the names of users and the dates of those orders are retrieved by this query.

Aggregation functions, such as COUNT, SUM, AVG, MAX, and MIN, are supported by SQL as well. These functions are used to calculate a single value from a set of variables. To group rows with the same values in designated columns into summary rows, these functions are frequently used in conjunction with the GROUP BY clause. For instance, you could type: {SELECT city, COUNT(*) FROM users GROUP BY city;} to get the total number of users in each city. This query counts the number of users in each city after grouping the users by town.

Moreover, groups formed by the GROUP BY clause are filtered using the HAVING clause. It functions on aggregated data and is comparable to the WHERE clause. For example, you could use {SELECT city, COUNT(*) FROM users GROUP BY city HAVING COUNT(*) > 10;} to locate towns with more than ten users.

In conclusion, SQL's fundamental syntax—specifically, the SELECT, FROM, and WHERE clauses—offers a solid and adaptable way to query databases. The FROM clause indicates which tables are involved, the SELECT clause lets you choose which columns to extract, and the WHERE clause filters the data according to predetermined criteria. To work with SQL and relational databases efficiently, gaining proficiency with these core elements is necessary, allowing users to derive valuable insights and make data-driven decisions. Comprehending these fundamentals establishes a solid basis in database administration and prepares the way for more sophisticated SQL procedures.

Filtering and Sorting Data

Fundamental SQL functions like filtering and sorting allow users to get particular subsets of data and arrange them logically. The WHERE clause, logical operators, the ORDER BY clause, and the LIMIT clause are the primary tools used to accomplish these actions. Anyone working with relational databases has to know how to use these clauses effectively.

The primary SQL filtering tool for data is the WHERE clause. Users can define requirements that must be fulfilled for rows to be incorporated into the result set. The WHERE clause requires the specification of a value, a comparison operator, and a column. For instance, the query `SELECT * FROM users WHERE age > 30;}` would be used to obtain all records from a user's table where the age exceeds 30. Data can be filtered with this clause according to several criteria, including date ranges, text matching, and numerical comparisons.

The WHERE clause's utility is improved with logical operators, which enable combining several conditions. AND, OR, and NOT are SQL's three leading logical operators. For a row to be included in the result set, the AND operator ensures that all required conditions are met. To find individuals who are over 30 and reside in New York, for example, run `SELECT * FROM users WHERE age > 30 AND city = 'New York';.` On the other hand, rows that satisfy at least one of the above conditions are included by the OR operator. As an illustration, the query {SELECT * FROM users WHERE age > 30 OR city = 'New York';} returns users who reside in New York or are older than 30. The NOT operator negates a condition by eliminating rows that satisfy the requirement. To extract all users except those who reside in New York, run `SELECT * FROM users WHERE NOT city = 'New York';.`

The WHERE clause allows pattern matching with the LIKE operator and wildcards in addition to standard comparisons. This is very helpful for text data filtering. The query `SELECT * FROM users WHERE name LIKE 'J%';,` for instance, returns people whose names begin with the letter 'J.' A single character is represented by the underscore (_), and any sequence of characters can be defined using the percent sign (%) wildcard. IN is an additional helpful operator that lets you specify several possible values for a column. One way to obtain users who reside in any of the mentioned cities is to execute the query `SELECT * FROM users WHERE city IN ('New York, Los Angeles, Chicago');.`

Sorting the findings is frequently required after data filtering to improve their meaning or facilitate analysis. For this, the ORDER BY clause is employed. Users can sort the result set in descending (DESC) or ascending (ASC) order based on one or more columns. If no order is supplied, the default is ascending. For instance, the query `SELECT * FROM users ORDER BY age ASC;} would be used to sort users by age in ascending order. The query `SELECT * FROM users ORDER BY age DESC;} would be used to sort by age in decreasing order. It is possible to specify more than one column for sorting, in which case the first column will sort the results first, followed by the remaining columns. For instance, `SELECT * FROM users ORDER BY age DESC, name ASC;` arranges the users first in ascending order by name for users of the same age and then in descending order by age.

The amount of rows returned in the result set can be limited using the LIMIT clause. This is very helpful when dealing with enormous datasets because it would be wasteful or inefficient to retrieve every entry. The LIMIT clause specifies the maximum number of rows to be returned. For instance, to extract only the top 10 entries from the user's table, use `SELECT * FROM users LIMIT 10:`. An OFFSET and the LIMIT clause can also define the beginning point at which the rows return. `SELECT * FROM users LIMIT 10 OFFSET 20;`, for example, finds ten rows beginning with the record that is 21. Applications that display results in pages frequently utilize pagination with this combination of LIMIT and OFFSET.

These clauses can be combined to provide robust and adaptable data retrieval. For instance, the query `SELECT name, age FROM users WHERE age > 30 ORDER BY age DESC LIMIT 10;}` might be used to obtain the names and ages of the first ten users over 30, sorted by age in descending order. This query restricts the result set to the first ten rows after removing individuals older than 30. The users are then sorted by age in descending order.

Highly personalized and effective queries can be created by combining the ORDER BY clause, LIMIT clause, and WHERE clause with logical operators. Take a sales database, for instance, with a sales table with columns for sale_date, amount, and customer_id. The following query would be used to obtain the top 5 sales from the previous month, sorted by the amount in decreasing order: {SELECT * FROM sales WHERE sale_date > '2023-05-01' ORDER BY amount DESC LIMIT 5;}. This search restricts the results to the top 5 sales and filters out any sales made after May 1, 2023. It also arranges the results by quantity in descending order.

These clauses can be used to suit specific criteria in more complicated cases. For instance, a subquery can locate the top 10 customers who have spent over $1000 in the past year, sorted by the total amount paid in descending order. This could be the significant question: {SELECT customer_id, total_spent SUM(amount) FROM sales WHERE sale_date > '2023-01-01' AND amount > 1000 GROUP BY customer_id ORDER BY total_spent DESC LIMIT 10;}. This query determines the total amount spent by each client, ranks the customers by the total amount paid in descending order, filters out sales more than $1000 made after January 1, 2023, groups the results by customer_id, and restricts the result set to the top 10 customers.

In conclusion, the WHERE clause, logical operators, the ORDER BY clause, and the LIMIT clause are crucial SQL strategies for filtering and sorting data. Logical operators that combine numerous conditions improve the WHERE clause's ability to perform exact filtering based on different circumstances. To make queries more effective and manageable, the LIMIT clause limits the number of rows returned, and the ORDER BY clause allows the result set to be sorted in a specified order. Gaining proficiency with these methods paves the way for more complex SQL querying and database administration by allowing users to retrieve, arrange, and evaluate data efficiently.

Aggregate Functions and Grouping

SQL's aggregate functions and grouping are essential ideas that let users compute data sets and arrange the results into informative summaries. In data analysis and reporting, these clauses and functions are frequently used to glean massive dataset insights. Each primary aggregate function—COUNT, SUM, AVG, MIN, and MAX— has a distinct function in data computing. Rows with a typical value can be grouped into summary rows using the GROUP BY clause, and groups can be filtered based on specific criteria using the HAVING clause.

The COUNT function is one of the most fundamental and often utilized aggregate functions in SQL. It gives back the total number of rows that satisfy a certain standard. To count all rows, use COUNT with an asterisk (*). Use COUNT with that column to count non-null values in a particular column. Examples of functions that return the overall number of employees are `SELECT COUNT(*) FROM employees;` and functions that return the number of employees with a non-null department ID are `SELECT COUNT(department_id) FROM employees;.` This method is beneficial for figuring out how big a dataset is or how often a particular value appears.

The SUM function determines the total sum of a numeric column. It is helpful for financial computations like adding up sales, revenues, or expenses. To compute the total salary expense for all employees, use {SELECT SUM(salary) FROM employees;`. The GROUP BY clause can be coupled with the SUM function to compute totals for various categories. To calculate the total salary expense for each department, for example, use `SELECT department_id, SUM(salary) FROM employees GROUP BY department_id;.`

The average value of a numerical column is calculated using the AVG function. Finding the mean value of data points, such as average sales, average scores, or average incomes, is a common usage for this function. To see the average wage of all employees, run {SELECT AVG(salary) FROM employees;`. When used in conjunction with the GROUP BY clause, the AVG function can reveal information about the average values within several groups. To compute the average salary for each department, for example, run `SELECT department_id, AVG(salary) FROM workers GROUP BY department_id;.`

The MIN and MAX methods can find the most minor and most significant values in a column. These routines are handy when finding extreme values in a dataset, like the highest and lowest scores, prices, or ages. In the employees table, for instance, `SELECT MIN(salary) FROM employees;` yields the lowest salary, and `SELECT MAX(salary) FROM employees;` yields the highest salary. When used with the GROUP BY clause, these functions can determine the minimum and maximum values within various groups. To get the lowest salary in each department, for instance, use `SELECT department_id, MIN(salary) FROM employees GROUP BY department_id;}; to find the highest salary in each department, use `SELECT department_id, MAX(salary) FROM employees GROUP BY department_id;}.

To group data according to one or more columns, the GROUP BY clause is necessary. It makes it possible to apply aggregate functions to each group separately, allowing for an in-depth examination of data subsets. The GROUP BY clause's primary syntax is to select which column or columns to group by following the main SELECT statement. For instance, `SELECT department_id, COUNT(*) FROM workers GROUP BY department_id;} counts the number of employees in each department after grouping them according to the department. More granular groupings can be created using the GROUP BY clause with several columns. For example, `SELECT department_id, job_id, COUNT(*) FROM workers GROUP BY department_id, job_id;` counts the number of employees in each combination of department and job after grouping them by both.

Groups formed by the GROUP BY clause can be filtered using the HAVING clause according to a given criterion. Like the WHERE clause, however, it works with data groups instead of individual rows. When it comes to excluding groups that don't fit particular requirements, the HAVING clause is helpful. To extract just departments with more than ten employees, for instance, run `SELECT department_id, COUNT(*) FROM employees GROUP BY department_id HAVING COUNT(*) > 10;`. Combine the

HAVING clause with aggregate functions to filter groups based on aggregated values. To extract just departments with an average pay of more than $50,000, for example, run `SELECT department_id, AVG(salary) FROM workers GROUP BY department_id HAVING AVG(salary) > 50000;`.

Data analysis that is both strong and thorough can be achieved by grouping and using aggregate functions. Take a sales database, for instance, with a sales table with columns for sale_date, amount, and product_id. The query `SELECT product_id, SUM(amount) FROM sales GROUP BY product_id;` would be used to get the total sales for each product. The total sales amount for each product is determined by grouping the sales by product ID in this query. An additional HAVING clause can be added to the query to limit further the results only to show products with total sales of more than $10,000: `SELECT product_id, SUM(amount) FROM sales GROUP BY product_id HAVING SUM(amount) > 10000;}.

A single query can employ Several aggregate functions to provide thorough insights in more complicated cases. For instance, the query would be: `SELECT product_id, SUM(amount) AS total_sales, AVG(amount) AS avg_sales, MIN(amount) AS min_sale, MAX(amount) AS max_sale FROM sales GROUP BY product_id;} to get the total, average, minimum, and maximum sales for each product. This query offers a comprehensive overview of sales information for every product, including the total sales amount, average sales amount, lowest sale amount, and most considerable sale amount.

The capacity to combine and aggregate data is necessary for data analysis, reporting, and decision-making. Users can also derive valuable insights from their data by utilizing the GROUP BY and HAVING clauses in conjunction with aggregate functions like COUNT, SUM, AVG, MIN, and MAX. By summarizing and filtering data according to different criteria, these strategies facilitate the identification of trends, patterns, and outliers. Anyone working with SQL and relational databases must understand these ideas to support well-informed decision-making processes and undertake sophisticated data analysis.

CHAPTER IV

Advanced SQL Queries

Subqueries and Nested Queries

Robust SQL features like subqueries and nested queries enable more intricate and dynamic data retrieval. A subquery is a SQL query inside another SQL query. It is sometimes referred to as an inner query or nested query. It is used to carry out frequently more compelling and complicated activities than what could be accomplished with a single query. Subqueries have distinct functions in different clauses, including SELECT, FROM, and WHERE. Furthermore, correlated subqueries are a unique subquery that further increases data retrieval versatility by referencing columns from the outer query.

Understanding subqueries is a step-by-step process. First, you need to grasp the concept of a subquery, which is essentially a query nested within another query and enclosed in parentheses. The outer query then uses the results of the subqueries that are conducted initially. Depending on the specifications of the outer query, subqueries can return a single value, a single row, several rows, or even a whole table. Subqueries can be used in different clauses of an SQL statement to perform a variety of operations, including data filtering, derived table creation, and computation.

The SELECT clause's usage of subqueries enables dynamic computations and data retrieval. Because it returns a single answer, this subquery is frequently called a scalar subquery. As an illustration, let's look at a sales database with a sales table, sale_id, sale_amount, and customer_id as columns. You might use the following subquery in the SELECT clause to discover the average sale amount for each sale: `SELECT sale_id, sale_amount, (SELECT AVG(sale_amount) FROM sales) AS avg_sale_amount FROM sales;}. The total average sale amount is determined by this query and is included in the result set for every row in the sales table.

To generate derived tables or temporary views that the outer query can query, subqueries can also be utilized in the FROM clause. This method works well for dissecting intricate queries into smaller, more digestible chunks. For instance, you could use the following subquery in the FROM clause to obtain the average sale amount by customer: `SELECT customer_id, AVG(sale_amount) AS avg_sale_amount FROM (SELECT customer_id, sale_amount FROM sales) AS customer_sales GROUP BY customer_id;}. The outer query in this query determines the average sale amount for each client, whereas the subquery collects the customer ID and sale value for each transaction.

Another popular location to employ subqueries is in the WHERE clause. WHERE clause subqueries are frequently used to filter data according to the output of another query, these subqueries are compatible with several comparison operators, including {={, {IN{, {ANY{, and {ALL}, and they can return one or more values. For instance, you could use the following subquery in the WHERE clause to locate sales made by customers who have made purchases above $500: `SELECT * FROM sales WHERE customer_id IN (SELECT customer_id FROM sales WHERE sale_amount > 500);}. This query retrieves all sales made by customers with sales larger than $500 after first identifying those customers.

A unique subquery called a correlated subquery uses columns from the outer query. Correlated subqueries are run once for every row of the outer query processes in contrast to ordinary ones. They are, therefore, more potent but may also require more resources. When processing rows one by one, related subqueries are frequently utilized when the value of a column in the outer query impacts the subquery. For instance, you could use the following correlated subquery to find sales where the sale amount is higher than the average sale amount for that customer's sales: `SELECT sale_id, sale_amount FROM sales AS s1 WHERE sale_amount > (SELECT AVG(sale_amount) FROM sales AS s2 WHERE s1.customer_id = s2.customer_id);}. This query gets sales that exceed the average amount by using a subquery to determine the average sale amount for each client.

Subqueries can be used with other SQL clauses and procedures to retrieve data in a highly customized and complicated manner. You could, for example, use a subquery with the ROW_NUMBER() function to find the top 3 highest sales for each customer: `SELECT sale_id, sale_amount, customer_id FROM (SELECT sale_id, sale_amount, customer_id, ROW_NUMBER() OVER (PARTITION BY customer_id ORDER BY sale_amount DESC) AS row_num FROM sales) AS ranked_sales WHERE row_num <= 3;}. The subquery in this query gives a row number to every sale made by each customer group, arranged in descending order of sale amount. The top three sales for each customer are the only results of the outer query.

The flexibility and power of SQL queries can be significantly increased using subqueries. They make it possible to create derived tables, calculate values dynamically, and do intricate filtering using several criteria. Subqueries should only be used sparingly, though, as they occasionally cause problems with performance, mainly when working with massive datasets or correlated subqueries that call for several executions. Subqueries' execution plans and optimization can help alleviate these performance worries.

In conclusion, SQL's nested queries and subqueries offer a reliable method for obtaining and manipulating complicated data. Subqueries can generate derived tables, perform dynamic calculations, and filter data according to intricate criteria in the SELECT, FROM, and WHERE clauses. Related subqueries provide even more flexibility by permitting row-by-row processing and allowing subqueries to reference columns from the outer query. Proficiency with subqueries is crucial for sophisticated SQL querying and can significantly improve your capacity to get insightful information from relational databases. To ensure effective and efficient data retrieval, like with any robust tool, it's crucial to employ subqueries effectively and consider any performance repercussions.

Joins

Joins are used in SQL to combine rows from one or more tables according to a shared column. In relational databases, joins are essential because they allow related data to be retrieved from many tables. There are various kinds of joins, each with a distinct function: self-joins, cross joins, inner joins, and outer joins (which include left, right, and full joins). Comprehending the various join types is vital for efficient database administration and intricate query development.

The most popular kind of joins are inner joins. Only the rows from the two join tables with matching values are returned. The result set of an inner join will be empty if there are no matches between the tables. An inner join's fundamental grammar is simple to understand: {SELECT table1.column = table2.column;` selects columns from table1 via an inner join with table2. For instance, you may execute the following SQL query to obtain all customers who have placed orders: `SELECT customers. Name, orders.order_id FROM customers INNER JOIN orders ON customers.customer_id = orders.customer_id;}. For clients who have placed orders alone, this query provides the customers' names and the order IDs that belong to them.

In contrast to inner joins, outside joins return both rows with matching values in both tables and rows without them. Outer joins come in three varieties: left, right, and full. All rows from the left table and the matched rows from the right table are returned by a left outer join, also known as a left join. The result is NULL on the right table's side if there is no match. {SELECT columns FROM table1 LEFT JOIN table2 ON table1.column = table2.column;} is the syntax for a left join. For example, you might use `SELECT customers—name, orders.order_id FROM customers LEFT JOIN orders ON customers.customer_id = orders.customer_id;` to extract all customers and their orders, including those who have not placed any orders. This query fills in NULL for customers without orders and returns all customers with their matching order IDs.

A right join is the opposite of a left join, sometimes known as a right outer join. The matching rows from the left table and every row from the right table are returned. The result is NULL on the left table's side if there is no match. {SELECT columns FROM table1 RIGHT JOIN table2 ON table1.column = table2.column;} is the syntax. A proper join using the same `customers` and `orders` tables would be: `SELECT customers. Name, orders.order_id FROM customers` to obtain all orders and their customers, including those orders without a corresponding customer (which is unusual in a well-designed database). Orders ON customers.customer_id = orders.customer_id;}RIGHT JOIN orders.

A full outer join returns all rows if there is a match in one of the tables. The outputs of the left and right outer joins are combined. On the side of the table without a match, the result is NULL if there isn't a match. {SELECT columns FROM table1 FULL OUTER JOIN table2 ON table1.column

= table2.column;` is the syntax. For example, you might use `SELECT customers. Name, orders.order_id FROM customers` to extract all customers and orders, including mismatched entries on both sides. Orders.customer_id = orders.customer_id;}FULL OUTER JOIN orders. When no matches exist, this query fills in NULLs and returns all customers and orders.

The Cartesian product of the two tables is returned by cross joins, sometimes referred to as Cartesian joins, and it contains every possible combination of rows from the tables. For matched rows, no conditions are stated. The syntax for a cross join is: `SELECT columns FROM table1 CROSS JOIN table2;`. For instance, you could use the following SQL query to list every possible product-category combination: `SELECT products—product_name, categories.category_name FROM products CROSS JOIN categories;`. This would involve having two tables, `products` and `categories.` This search yields all conceivable combinations of categories and goods.

To join a table with itself, use self-joins. When comparing rows inside the same table or retrieving hierarchical data is required, this can be helpful. Table aliases are necessary to differentiate between the instances of the table in the query when doing a self-join. While the syntax is the same as other joins, aliases are used: {SELECT *, *, * FROM table an INNER JOIN table b ON a.common_column = b.common_column;}. Take a look at a `employees} table, for instance, where the columns {employee_id}, `name}, and `manager_id} are employee_id}, manager_id} being a reference to another employee-id}. You would use a self-join to obtain the names of the employees and their managers: {SELECT e1.name AS employee, e2.name AS manager FROM employees e1.manager_id = e2.employee_id;{.e1 INNER JOIN employees e2. This query joins the table to retrieve employees and their corresponding managers.

Every kind of join has a distinct function and works well in various situations. Inner joins are great for getting matched data from linked tables, ensuring that only relevant rows are returned. Outer joins are helpful when you need to include unmatched data since they offer a more complete view of the dataset. When you need to list all customers regardless of whether they have placed orders, for example, or when you need to include all data from a primary table, even if there are no matches in the associated table, left joins come in handy. Full outer joins offer a comprehensive set of results by integrating the advantages of both left and right joins, while right joins are less frequently utilized but can be helpful in reverse cases.

Cross joins are beneficial in some analytical contexts and can be effective at creating combinations, but if not utilized appropriately, they can result in substantial result sets. However, self-joins are essential for comparing rows within the same table or querying hierarchical data, allowing for sophisticated data linkages and insights.

It's essential to comprehend the subtleties of these joins and know when to apply each kind for effective database management and querying. When joins are correctly used, accurate and efficient data retrieval is ensured, supporting intricate data analysis and decision-making procedures. Anyone dealing with SQL and relational databases must have a solid understanding of joins to fully utilize these systems' capabilities and extract insightful and valuable information from their data.

Set Operations

You can create a single result set in SQL by combining the output of two or more queries using set operations. These operations—UNION, UNION ALL, INTERSECT, and EXCEPT—are founded on the ideas of set theory. These operations are valuable tools for sophisticated data retrieval and processing since they have unique properties and use cases.

Duplicate rows are removed when combining the output of two or more SELECT operations into a single result set using the UNION procedure. There must be equal columns in the result sets with comparable data types for each SELECT statement inside the UNION. The UNION syntax is simple to understand: SELECT table1; column 1; column 2 UNIONE SELECT table2; column1, column2;. To generate a list of all unique customers from both nations, you could use the following query: SELECT customer_id, customer_name FROM us_customers. This would allow you to have tables of customers from the United States and Canada. UNIONE SELECT customer_id, customer_name FROM canada_customers;. A list of distinct customers from both tables—duplicates removed—is produced by this query.

Like UNION, UNION ALL comprises all rows—including duplicates—from the SELECT statement result sets. This operation comes in handy when you want to incorporate every instance of data—regardless of whether it occurs in many result sets. SELECT column1, column2 FROM table1 is the syntax. FROM table2, UNION ALL SELECT column1, column2;. You could use the following, for instance, to obtain a full list of customers from the US and Canada databases, including any duplicates: SELECT customer_id, customer_name FROM us_customers UNION ALL SELECT customer_name, customer_id FROM canada_customers;. All customers are included in this query, which flags duplication when a client occurs in multiple tables.

Only the rows shared by the result sets of two or more SELECT queries are returned by the INTERSECT operation. By displaying only the overlapping data, it successfully executes an intersection of the datasets.

INTERSECT has the following syntax: SELECT column1, column2 FROM table1. INTERSECT SELECT table2; column1, column2;. For example, you might use the following query to locate customers who are included in both the US and Canada tables: SELECT customer_id, customer_name FROM us_customers From canada_customers, do an intersect choose to select for customer_id and customer_name. Only the clients specified in both tables are returned by this query.

The rows from the first select statement absent from the second select statement's result set are returned by the EXCEPT operation, sometimes referred to as MINUS in some SQL dialects. This function helps identify variations between datasets. To use EXCEPT, type this syntax: SELECT column1, column2 FROM table1. SEPARATE column1, column2 FROM table2; is not allowed. To locate consumers in the US table but not in the Canada table, for instance, you could use the following query: SELECT customer_id, customer_name FROM us_customers OTHER THAN SELECT customer_id, customer_name FROM canada_customers;. This query returns customers exclusive to the US table; those from the Canada table are not included.

Several guidelines and best practices govern set operations to guarantee proper and effective utilization. A crucial guideline is that every select statement's columns must have an equal number and comparable data types. Furthermore, parenthesis can be used to modify the evaluation order or to make complex queries more understandable. Set operations are evaluated from left to right. SELECT column1, column2 FROM table1 UNION SELECT column1, column2 FROM table2) INTERSECT SELECT column1, column2 FROM table3; is an example of how to combine UNION and INTERSECT procedures.

When combining, comparing, or contrasting datasets is required, set procedures are helpful. For example, a company may use EXCEPT to find consumers unique to a specific region, INTERSECT to find customers who have purchased in numerous areas, and UNION to combine client lists from different regions. Queries that would otherwise need intricate joins and conditional expressions can be made simpler with the help of these techniques.

In some circumstances, using set operations can also enhance query performance. For example, when merging big datasets with comparable structures, a UNION operation may be more effective than a sequence of JOINs. Nonetheless, it's critical to understand the possible effects of set operations on performance, especially when dealing with big datasets. Because UNION ALL does not necessitate the removal of duplicates, it is typically faster than UNION and is a preferable option when duplicate data is permitted.

Set operations can be applied to various data manipulation activities in real-world scenarios. Set operations, for example, can be used in data warehousing to combine data from several source systems into a single perspective. They can be used to create thorough reports in reporting and analytics that compile data from various periods or categories. Set operations can be used in database migrations to find differences between source and target systems and guarantee data completeness and consistency.

Imagine a business wishing to combine multiple regional databases into a single customer database. Each customer record from each regional database can be merged into a single dataset by the company using UNION, guaranteeing that each client is listed once. INTERSECT can locate familiar clients across regional databases if the company also wishes to identify customers who have engaged with different regions. On the other hand, EXCEPT offers insights into local consumer bases by assisting with identifying clients exclusive to a given area.

A further real-world example concerns personnel files. Assume a company keeps separate records for its previous and present workers. UNION may merge the current and historical employee tables to get an exhaustive list of everyone who has ever worked for the company. INTERSECT can locate workers who have changed from their current to their previous status by identifying those in both tables. By comparing the present workforce with the entire list of all employees, EXCEPT can be used to identify former employees.

To sum up, set operations in SQL, such as INTERSECT, EXCEPT, UNION, and UNION ALL, offer strong capabilities for merging, contrasting, and comparing information. Complex data retrieval and manipulation require these operations to enable effective and efficient data analysis. Users can enhance efficiency, obtain a more profound understanding of their data, and simplify their queries through comprehension and implementation of set operations. Anyone dealing with SQL and relational databases must be proficient in set operations. This will improve their capacity to manage and analyze data in various dynamic contexts.

CHAPTER V

Data Manipulation

Inserting Data

Adding new data to a database in SQL is accomplished with the INSERT INTO statement. This statement is vital to updating and maintaining the data kept in a database and the process of adding data to tables. Depending on the requirements of the database operations, the INSERT INTO statement can be used in various ways, such as inserting a single row, numerous rows, or even bulk inserts. It is essential to comprehend the subtleties of these techniques to maintain databases effectively and guarantee data integrity.

The INSERT INTO statement has simple syntax at its core. It permits one row of data to be inserted into a designated table. {INSERT INTO table_name (column1, column2, column3,...) VALUES (value1, value2, value3,...);` is the syntax. Look at a table called `employees}, for instance, which has the columns `employee_id}, `first_name}, and `last_name}. The following line might be used to insert a single row into this table: {INSERT INTO workers (employee_id, first_name, last_name) VALUES (1, 'John,' 'Doe');}. This command creates a new employee record with the values for each supplied column.

Inserting numerous rows at once is another technique to use the INSERT INTO statement. To accomplish this, add more sets of values to the VALUES clause and separate them with commas. {INSERT INTO table_name (column1, column2, column3,...) VALUES (value1, value2, value3,...), (value4, value5, value6,...),...;} is the syntax for this. For instance, you could type: {INSERT INTO employees (employee_id, first_name, last_name)

VALUES (2, 'Jane,' 'Smith'), (3, 'Robert,' 'Brown'), (4, 'Emily,' 'Johnson');} to insert several employee records into the `employees` table. Adding three new rows to the {employees` table with this command is more effective than inserting each row separately.

The INSERT INTO statement can be used to insert data from another table and directly insert data. This is very helpful for transferring data between databases or moving data from one table to another. INSERT INTO table_name (column1, column2, column3,...) is the syntax for this method. SELECT (condition) FROM another_table, column1, column2, column3,... For instance, you might write: `INSERT INTO employees (employee_id, first_name, last_name) SELECT employee_id, first_name, last_name FROM new_employees;} if you had a table called `new_employees` and you wanted to replicate all of its data into the `employees` table. The `new_employees` table's rows are all selected by this command, which then adds them to the `employees` table.

An advanced version of the INSERT INTO statement called a bulk insert is used to insert enormous amounts of data effectively. For jobs like data migration, batch processing, and data loading into a data warehouse, bulk inserts are necessary. Bulk insert efficiency is attained by streamlining the data insertion process and cutting overhead related to several single-row insert processes. Different database management systems (DBMS) offer different tools and techniques for carrying out bulk inserts. For example, in SQL Server, data can be loaded into a table from a file using the `BULK INSERT` command. {BULK INSERT table_name FROM 'file_path' WITH (options);` is the syntax. For example, you could write: `BULK INSERT employees FROM 'C:\\data\\employees.csv' WITH (FIELDTERMINATOR =," ROWTERMINATOR = '\n');} to import data from a CSV file into the `employees` table. Using commas to divide fields and newlines to separate rows, this program takes data from the CSV file and inserts it into the `employees` database.

Using MySQL's `LOAD DATA INFILE` statement is another popular technique for large data inserting. This operation is quite effective for loading huge datasets from a file into a table. {LOAD DATA INFILE 'file_path' INTO TABLE table_name FIELDS TERMINATED BY 'delimiter' LINES TERMINATED BY 'line_terminator';} is the syntax. `LOAD DATA INFILE '/path/to/employees.csv' INTO TABLE employees FIELDS TERMINATED BY, " LINES TERMINATED BY '\n';} is one example of how to load data from a CSV file into the `employees` table. Using commas to divide fields and newlines to separate rows, this program takes data from the CSV file and puts it into the table.

When executing bulk inserts, it is imperative to consider the possible effects on database integrity and performance. Performance bottlenecks may arise from bulk adding vast amounts of data, especially if the database is busy or the target table has a lot of constraints and indexes. It is frequently advised to temporarily turn off constraints and indexes before executing bulk inserts and re-enable them afterward to minimize these problems. Ensuring the data being entered complies with the table's schema and restrictions is crucial to avoid data corruption and preserve data integrity.

Transaction management is still another essential factor to consider when doing bulk inserts. By using transactions, you can ensure that the bulk insert process is handled as a single atomic unit that can be undone in case of an error. This methodology contributes to preserving data integrity and consistency, especially when inconsistent data could result from partial data inclusion. For example, in SQL Server, you may wrap a bulk insert operation within a transaction as follows: `BEGIN TRANSACTION; BULK INSERT employees FROM 'C:\\data\\employees.csv' WITH (FIELDTERMINATOR =," ROWTERMINATOR = '\n'); COMMIT TRANSACTION;.` By doing this, the database's integrity is maintained, and either all the data is successfully inserted, or none is.

In conclusion, adding data to a database may be accomplished with the help of the flexible and robust SQL INSERT INTO statement. Database management efficiency depends on knowing how to use this statement correctly, whether entering one row, several rows, or bulk inserts. While multi-row inserts provide a more practical approach to adding several entries simultaneously, single-row inserts are simple and helpful for adding individual records. Large amounts of data must be handled efficiently, and several DBMSs offer specific commands and techniques for bulk inserts. To preserve the consistency and dependability of the database, bulk inserts must take transaction management and data integrity into account. To efficiently populate and maintain databases, database administrators and developers must master using the INSERT INTO statement and its variations.

Updating Data

Mastering the art of maintaining and controlling the correctness and applicability of information in a database is a powerful skill. The SQL UPDATE statement is the key to this power, as it allows you to change records that are already in the table. This process can be as simple as updating specific columns directly, or it can be more involved and involve using subqueries to find the new values for those columns. As database administrators and developers, your ability to guarantee data consistency and integrity over time is directly linked to your proficiency with the UPDATE statement and its subqueries.

The table to be updated, the column or columns to be changed, and the new values for those columns are the essential components of the UPDATE statement's syntax. The formula is as follows: {UPDATE table_name SET condition; where column1 = value1, column2 = value2;}. Consider the following scenario: you wish to offer one employee with a particular ID a 10% raise and have a table called `employees` with the columns `salary` and `employee_id}. {UPDATE workers SET salary = salary * 1.10 WHERE employee_id = 101;} would be the SQL statement. With this command, the employee with {employee_id~ 101's salary is updated in the `salary` column, showing a 10% increase.

The WHERE clause is one of the most crucial components of the UPDATE statement. The criteria that must be satisfied for a row to be updated are specified in the WHERE clause. The UPDATE statement would apply to every row in the table if there were no WHERE clause, which could have unforeseen and potentially fatal consequences. For example, in the above example, if you remove the WHERE clause, all the employees in the `employees` table would receive a 10% raise: `UPDATE employees SET salary = salary * 1.10;}. It is crucial to use the WHERE clause carefully to update only the intended rows.

The UPDATE statement can use subqueries and straightforward updates to find the new column values. Nestled queries called subqueries supply the data that the outer query needs. Subqueries can execute calculations depending on other rows in the same table or retrieve values from different tables when utilized in an UPDATE statement. Because of this, subqueries are practical tools for complex updates requiring conditional logic or data from several sources.

When a SELECT statement is used in a UPDATE statement, it is embedded within either the SET or WHERE clauses. Take a hypothetical situation where you have two tables, `employees} and `departments,` where `employees` contains the values `department_id} and `salary} and `departments` contains the values `department_id} and `budget}. You can use the following subquery to adjust an employee's {salary} based on their department's budget: `adjust employees SET salary = salary * 1.05 WHERE department_id = (SELECT department_id FROM departments WHERE budget > 100000);}. Due to this directive, employees who work in departments with budgets over $100,000 are eligible for a 5% rise.

Subqueries can also be utilized in the SET clause to retrieve values from other tables. Assume, for instance, that you wish to update the {department_id} of workers according to the `department_name} from a different table named `department_changes}, which contains a list of newly assigned departments. "UPDATE employees SET department_id = (SELECT new_department_id FROM department_changes   WHERE department_changes.employee_id   = employees.employee_id);" is the SQL statement that would be used. Using the matching entry from the `department_changes` database as a basis, this command modifies the `department_id} for every employee.

Utilizing subqueries in updates for conditional updates based on aggregated data is another helpful application. To increase the `bonus` column in the `employees` table for salespersons who have achieved above-average sales, for example, in a table {sales} with columns {salesperson_id} and `total_sales}, you can use the following subquery to calculate the average sales and apply the update: `UPDATE employees SET bonus = bonus + 1000 WHERE employee_id IN (SELECT salesperson_id FROM sales WHERE total_sales > (SELECT AVG(total_sales) FROM sales));}. With this command, employees with sales over average receive an additional bonus.

Subqueries give a UPDATE statement a great deal of flexibility and power, enabling complicated updates that can consider various situations and data sources. But there are also performance concerns that need to be carefully considered. Subqueries occasionally result in inefficient queries, mainly when several nested subqueries or big tables are involved. To improve performance, it is crucial to optimize queries and make sure that indexes are used effectively.

Furthermore, data integrity requires using transactions in conjunction with the UPDATE statement. Through transactions, multiple updates are handled as a single atomic operation, ensuring that in case of a mistake, all updates are applied or none. This is especially crucial for intricate upgrades that incorporate numerous tables or conditions. For instance, you can utilize transactions in SQL Server like this: {BEGIN TRANSACTION; UPDATE employees SET salary = salary * 1.10 WHERE employee_id = 101; COMMIT TRANSACTION;}. This guarantees that the change will only be committed if every transactional process is successful.

In conclusion, the SQL UPDATE statement is an effective tool for changing already-existing data in a database. Knowing the complete capabilities of the UPDATE statement is crucial for efficient database management, whether you're updating a few selected columns or utilizing intricate subqueries to find new values. Subqueries allow you to combine data from different sources and conditions, while the WHERE clause guarantees that only the required rows are updated. To preserve data integrity, transactions must be used, and performance factors must also be considered. Database managers and developers can guarantee that their databases stay correct, current, and effective by becoming proficient with the UPDATE statement and its numerous applications.

Deleting Data

One of the most critical operations for controlling the lifespan of data in a database is deleting data in SQL. Ensuring that sensitive, irrelevant, or out-of-date material is eliminated through proper data deletion preserves the effectiveness and security of the database. The DELETE and TRUNCATE statements are the two main SQL procedures for deleting data. Although the goal of both commands is to remove data, they differ significantly in terms of how they are used, how well they work, and how they affect the structure of the database.

The DELETE statement is employed when removing particular rows from a table according to a WHERE clause condition. The DELETE FROM table_name WHERE condition is the fundamental syntax of the DELETE statement. The rows that are eliminated can be precisely controlled using this command. DELETE FROM workers WHERE contract_end_date < '2023-01-01'; is one such query to use, for instance, if you have a database called "employees" and wish to remove the records of employees whose contracts have expired. Only those rows with a contract expiration date before January 1, 2023, are eliminated by this command.

The versatility of the DELETE statement is one of its main advantages. In the WHERE clause, you can precisely pinpoint which rows should be eliminated by providing conditions. If the WHERE clause is absent, the DELETE statement removes every row from the table. Unlike the TRUNCATE statement, it does so row by row while preserving the table's structure and metadata, including the values and indexes of the identity columns. This method may be helpful When you selectively remove data while maintaining the table's schema and indexes.

Joins and subqueries can also be used with the DELETE statement to fine-tune the deletion criteria further. For example, you could use DELETE FROM workers WHERE department_id IN (SELECT department_id FROM departments WHERE status = 'closed') to remove people from the "employees" table who are in closed departments. Only employees who are associated with closed departments are deleted by this command.

Additionally, in many SQL databases, like PostgreSQL, the DELETE command offers the RETURNING clause, which can be used to return the removed records. This function is handy for operations like DELETE FROM workers WHERE contract_end_date < '2023-01-01' RETURNING *, that need the data before it can be deleted, or for auditing purposes. The specified rows are removed with this command, which also gives the deleted rows' information.

When utilizing the DELETE statement, transactions are essential. A DELETE operation can be ensured to be atomic, consistent, isolated, and durable (ACID characteristics) by including it in a transaction. This implies that the transaction can be rolled back, returning the database to its initial state if an error arises during the deletion process. In SQL Server, for example, you may use the following commands: BEGIN TRANSACTION; DELETE FROM workers WHERE contract_end_date < '2023-01-01'; COMMIT; You can use ROLLBACK; to undo a transaction if something goes wrong.

However, the TRUNCATE command can swiftly and effectively remove every row from a table. The syntax is less complicated: TABLE TRUNCATE table_name;. Since TRUNCATE removes every row in the table in a single atomic action, it does not require a WHERE clause like DELETE. For instance, you might use TRUNCATE database workers to eliminate every row from the "employees" database.

Performance is the main benefit of TRUNCATE over DELETE. Due to its ability to deallocate the data pages the table uses, thereby returning it to its initial empty state without documenting individual row removals, TRUNCATE is typically faster. Because TRUNCATE logs fewer rows deleted, it is more efficient for large tables than DELETE, which logs each row deletion separately. It can also be executed much faster due to its reduced logging.

The fact that TRUNCATE doesn't trigger triggers is another significant distinction. When you use TRUNCATE, any triggers set up for DELETE operations in your table will not activate. When you wish to swiftly remove a table without triggering the overhead of trigger execution, this behavior may be helpful. That implies that no business logic contained in those triggers will be carried out.

Additionally, TRUNCATE resets any identity columns in the database, so the initial declared value will be used for the next insert operation. On the other hand, DELETE keeps the value sequence intact because it does not reset identity columns. When the identity value sequence is critical for your application, it is vital to consider this difference.

In contrast to DELETE, TRUNCATE has certain drawbacks despite its performance advantages. TRUNCATE cannot be applied when a foreign key constraint references a table. An error will occur if you try to truncate a table with foreign critical dependencies. Furthermore, DELETE usually only needs DELETE permission on the table, but TRUNCATE usually requires higher rights, frequently needing the user to have the ALTER TABLE permission.

Which option to use—DELETE or TRUNCATE—depends on your database operation's particular needs and limitations. DELETE is the right option if you need to execute related business logic, have fine-grained control over the deletion process, or remove specific rows depending on circumstances. DELETE offers the required accuracy, for instance, if you need to erase records of employees who left the organization before a particular date while keeping the rest of the data.

On the other hand, TRUNCATE is a preferable choice if you need to swiftly erase all of the data in a table to start over or if you need to rapidly delete a lot of data without considering any row-specific criteria or triggers. This method works well for tasks like cleaning up logs, resetting staging tables, or carrying out bulk deletions in data warehousing settings when trigger absence and identity sequence reset are not problems.

To sum up, each SQL command, DELETE and TRUNCATE, with specific advantages and suitable applications, is indispensable for extracting data from tables. With its precision and versatility, the DELETE statement supports transactions, conditional deletions, and trigger-based business logic triggering. By moving data pages and resetting identity columns, TRUNCATE offers better speed for mass deletions; however, foreign fundamental limitations and permission levels must be carefully considered. Comprehending the distinctions of these commands and their consequences is essential for the proficient management of databases, guaranteeing data accuracy and enhancing efficiency. Database administrators and developers can effectively handle data deletion duties while preserving their databases' general health and operation by using the appropriate command, depending on the situation.

CHAPTER VI

Data Definition Language (DDL)

Creating Tables and Schemas

One of the fundamental tasks of database management is creating tables and schemas, which are necessary for efficiently storing, retrieving, and manipulating data by organizing and structuring it. A crucial command in this process is CREATE TABLE, which allows database administrators and developers to specify data types for each column, define a table's structure, and impose constraints to guarantee data integrity. Furthermore, schema creation offers a higher level of structure within a database by putting related tables and other objects under a shared namespace.

The first step In creating a new table in a database is to execute the CREATE TABLE statement. This command defines the name of the table, the columns in it, and the data types for each of those columns. The data types determine the types of data that can be stored in each column—integers, floating-point numbers, texts, dates, and more. For instance, a table storing customer data might have columns for the customer's ID, name, email address, and birthdate, each with the data types DATE, VARCHAR, and INTEGER. `CREATE TABLE customers (customer_id INTEGER, name VARCHAR(100), email VARCHAR(100), birthdate DATE);} may be the SQL syntax for constructing such a table. The data type follows the name of each column in each definition. Selecting the right kind of data is essential since it determines how it is kept, how much space it takes up, and what actions can be taken.

Another crucial component of the CREATE TABLE statement is specifying constraints. The Rules applied to the data to guarantee accuracy and consistency are called constraints. Constraints with the following common names are: PRIMARY KEY, FOREIGN KEY, UNIQUE, NOT NULL, and CHECK. The PRIMARY KEY constraint uniquely identifies every record in a table. For example, the primary key in the customer's table might be defined as the customer_id column with the syntax {PRIMARY KEY (customer_id)}. Guaranteeing that every customer_id value is distinct and not null offers a dependable method of identifying individual data. Referential integrity is enforced via the FOREIGN KEY constraint, which creates a relationship between two tables. A FOREIGN KEY constraint can be applied, for instance, if the customer_id column in the orders table references the customer's table. This will guarantee that each customer_id in the orders table corresponds to a valid customer_id in the customers table. {FOREIGN KEY (customer_id) REFERENCES customers(customer_id)} may be the syntax for this. While NOT NULL constraints prevent null values in defined columns and CHECK constraints enforce specific criteria, such {CHECK (age >= 18)} to ensure that age values are at least 18, UNIQUE constraints guarantee that all values in a column are distinct.

Creating schemas is another essential step in database design that offers a higher level of organization. A schema assembles database components under a common name, such as tables, views, indexes, and procedures. These objects are logically grouped with schemas, facilitating database maintenance, permission management, and comprehension of the connections between various database components. For instance, in an extensive application, data about orders, items, and customers may be divided using multiple schemas. In SQL, constructing a schema is simple: `CREATE SCHEMA sales;` generates a new schema with the name sales. By giving the schema name, such as `CREATE TABLE sales. Customers (customer_id INTEGER, name VARCHAR(100), email VARCHAR(100), birthdate DATE);}, tables, and other objects can be constructed within the schema once it has been built.

Effective schema use necessitates meticulous organization and planning. Schemas can represent several application functional areas, divide data for various customers in a multi-tenant system, and segregate development and testing environments from production. Schemas are essential for object organization and for managing rights and security. Database administrators can manage access to all objects inside a schema and streamline providing and rescinding access by assigning permissions at the schema level. To improve data security, access to a schema containing sensitive data, for example, might be limited to people who need it.

The CREATE TABLE statement and schema generation are closely related in database design and management. They serve as the framework for a secure, effective, and well-organized database system. The selection of data types and constraints for every table and the overall schema layout should be carefully considered when building a new database. Data is efficiently stored, and the database can execute required operations fast when data types are defined correctly. Data integrity is upheld by constraints, which stop erroneous data from entering the database and guarantee the preservation of table relationships. Schemas improve the database's usability and security by offering a logical foundation for managing and organizing database objects.

Defining the structure and organization of the data entails building tables and schemas, which is an essential part of database management. The CREATE TABLE statement lays the foundation for data integrity and adequate storage, which enables the specification of columns, data types, and constraints. By combining similar database objects into schemas, you may add another level of organization and make permissions management easier. These components work together to provide a robust, organized database system that can handle the intricate data requirements of contemporary applications. To ensure that the database satisfies present needs and is flexible enough to accommodate future modifications, thorough planning and execution of these tasks are necessary.

Altering Tables

Changing tables is a fundamental database management procedure that is essential to maintain and adapt a database's structure as needs evolve over time. The operations of ADD, DROP, and MODIFY columns, as well as altering data types, are at the heart of this procedure. Each operation has distinct use cases and can significantly impact data integrity and overall database performance, underscoring the need for a comprehensive understanding and careful execution.

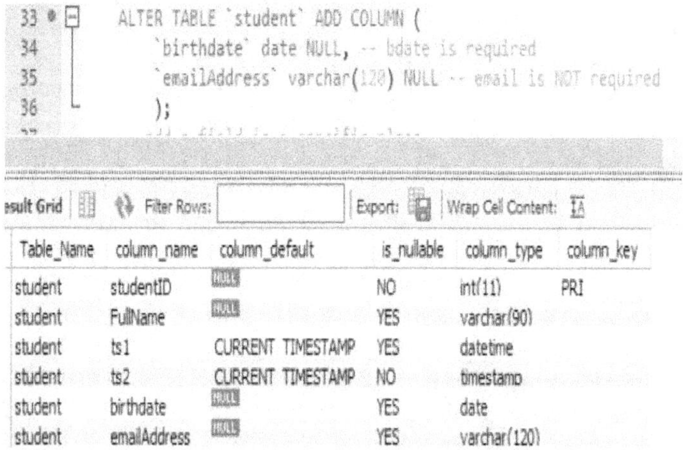

Table_Name	column_name	column_default	is_nullable	column_type	column_key
student	studentID	NULL	NO	int(11)	PRI
student	FullName	NULL	YES	varchar(90)	
student	ts1	CURRENT_TIMESTAMP	YES	datetime	
student	ts2	CURRENT_TIMESTAMP	NO	timestamp	
student	birthdate	NULL	YES	date	
student	emailAddress	NULL	YES	varchar(120)	

The ADD procedure is utilized when additional columns need to be added to an existing table. This can be necessary when more data properties are required to collect more information. For example, an ADD operation might create a new column in a customer database to hold the client's birthday if the company decides to start keeping track of them. The table name and the specifics of the new column, such as its name and data type, must be specified in the syntax for this operation. The command could seem like this in SQL: {ALTER TABLE customers ADD birthdate DATE;}. This command instructs the database management system to update the `customers` table by adding a new column called `birthdate` with the data type {DATE}. Ensuring that the new columns don't breach any current data integrity requirements is one of the main things to keep in mind while adding new columns. A default value can be needed if a NOT NULL constraint is applied to the new column to avoid the process failing because of existing rows and would otherwise have NULL values for the new column.

In contrast, the DROP procedure can eliminate a table's columns. This may be required if some columns become obsolete due to a database redesign or specific data properties are no longer needed. For instance, the DROP action can delete a column that once held temporary calculation results but is no longer necessary. This operation has a simple syntax, like `ALTER TABLE customers DROP COLUMN temporary_result;}. However, removing a column might have serious repercussions, mainly if other database components like views, triggers, or stored procedures refer to it. Furthermore, data saved in the discarded column is permanently destroyed; therefore, careful thought and a data backup are advised before this procedure.

To modify an existing column's definition, use the MODIFY procedure. This could entail modifying restrictions, changing the default value, or changing the data type. For example, the data type of an integer-storing column may be modified from `INT}` to {BIGINT} if the column has to hold larger values. An example command for this could be {ALTER TABLE customers MODIFY age BIGINT;}. The syntax for this can vary. It can be difficult to change the data type of a column, especially if the new data type is incompatible with the old one. For example, changing a column from `VARCHAR` to `INT}` may fail if it contains non-numeric values. Furthermore, modifications to constraints—like making a column NOT NULL—may require that every database record match the updated constraint. This could mean that more data-cleaning procedures will be needed before the ALTER TABLE command can be run appropriately.

One particular type of MODIFY operation that needs careful consideration is changing the data types. The data types that can be stored in a column are determined by their data types, including string, date and time, numeric, and more. A column's data type may need to be changed for several reasons, including enhanced performance, support for larger values, or fixing early design errors. For instance, a column called {TINYINT{ may need to be modified to `INT}` or {BIGINT{ if it was initially intended to hold smaller integers but needs to accommodate more significant values as a result of business expansion. Altering the data type of a column usually follows the same syntax as other MODIFY operations, such as `ALTER TABLE orders MODIFY order_id BIGINT;}`. But considerable preparation is needed for this operation. It is necessary to consider compatibility between old and new data formats and potential problems with data conversion. For example, to convert a `VARCHAR}` column to a `DATE}`, all current values must be valid dates; otherwise, the conversion process will fail or result in lost data.

Each of these operations impacts the database schema— ADD, DROP, MODIFY columns, and changing data types—

and these changes can also significantly affect storage, application compatibility, and database performance. It's crucial to consider how additional columns will be used and whether or not they will introduce redundancy or go against normalization standards before adding them and using caution while dropping columns is essential so that no dependencies or essential data are lost. When modifying columns and switching data types, it is necessary to understand the present data and how the changes would impact it thoroughly.

These actions are not just theoretical concepts, but practical tools frequently used by database administrators as a part of optimization and migration efforts. For instance, schema modifications may be necessary during a migration to a new system or version to leverage new database features or conform to new application requirements. Similarly, performance enhancement may involve changing columns to more efficient data types, indexing newly added columns, or removing unnecessary columns to optimize storage. This practical application of the procedures underscores their relevance and importance in real-world database management.

In conclusion, one crucial aspect of database administration that empowers the schema to adapt to evolving business demands is the ability to change tables using the ADD, DROP, and MODIFY columns, along with the data types that are used. The meticulous planning and consideration required for these actions underscore the pivotal role of database administrators and IT professionals in ensuring data integrity, application compatibility, and performance. When executed with precision, these procedures enable the database to continue meeting the needs of the organization effectively and efficiently.

Dropping Tables and Databases

The SQL procedures DROP TABLE and DROP DATABASE are not just tools for eliminating data structures, they are crucial for maintaining a functional and effective database system. Understanding the consequences, syntax, and use cases of these procedures is paramount to prevent potential data loss and ensure the smooth operation of your database.

The DROP TABLE statement can remove an existing table and its contents from a database. Because of the irreversible nature of this operation, all data included in a dropped table is lost forever unless it was previously backed up. This operation has the following simple syntax: {DROP TABLE table_name;}. For example, the command `DROP TABLE employees;` would eliminate the table {employees` from the database if it was no longer needed. The table's related constraints, triggers, permissions, and indexes are likewise eliminated during this procedure. Since this operation is permanent, it is usually advised to back up the data or confirm that the table is no longer required before running it. Database administrators must also be aware of any dependent objects or programs that might depend on the table being discarded.

It may be required to drop a table for several reasons. For instance, some tables may become redundant when data is combined or normalized during database optimization or redesign. Similarly, tables temporarily generated for preliminary calculations or reports may be removed when they fulfill their intended function. Cleaning up after a migration when legacy tables are no longer needed is another typical case. You should always thoroughly consider and plan before removing a table to prevent unintentional data loss or application issues.

In contrast, a complete database and all of its components—tables, views, indexes, stored procedures, and other objects—can be deleted with the DROP DATABASE statement. Since it deletes every piece of information and object in the designated database, this command has significantly more of an impact than the DROP TABLE. This command likewise has a straightforward syntax: `DROP DATABASE database_name;}. For instance, the command `DROP DATABASE sales_db;} might remove a database named `sales_db}. This operation is irrevocable and must be done carefully, just like dropping a table. Before moving forward, it is imperative to confirm that the database is no longer required or that a complete backup is in place.

In certain situations, it may be required to drop a database. For testing purposes, several databases may be built in a development environment. These databases can be removed to free up resources after testing is over. Similarly, during system upgrades or decommissioning, databases connected to out-of-date applications or data structures may be eliminated in a production environment. To prevent mistakes or disruptions, database administrators must ensure that no active connections are utilizing the database that is about to be discarded. Before abandoning a database, most database management systems include tools to examine and end active connections if needed.

The DROP TABLE and DROP DATABASE statements are practical tools for managing database settings but using them wisely and in advance calls for preparation. Since these commands are irreversible, any error could result in a substantial loss of data and cause business activities to be disrupted. Thus, it's crucial to have protections in place, like frequent backups, in-depth impact analyses, and change management procedures. Furthermore, by delivering confirmation dialogs and dependency checks, database management tools that give visual interfaces for these processes can assist in lowering the chance of errors.

The lifecycle of databases and tables is frequently managed by automated scripts and tools in contemporary database management methods. These scripts may have checks and balances to guarantee that dropping actions are carried out safely. Scripts may comprise procedures such as confirming that a database or table is not being used, ensuring a backup, and logging the operation for auditing purposes. These procedures aid in preserving the database environment's dependability and integrity.

Furthermore, version control systems are increasingly being used for database schemas. In these systems, version-controlled scripts are used to track and manage modifications to the database schema, such as removing tables and databases. This method ensures that changes are recorded, makes it easier for teams to work together on database modifications, and offers a way to undo changes if needed. Organizations can improve the consistency and dependability of their database management procedures by combining version control with automated deployment pipelines.

To sum up, the SQL commands DROP TABLE and DROP DATABASE are essential for deleting tables and databases. Since these actions are irreversible, care must be taken to prevent accidental data loss. While dropping databases is required to decommission complete database setups, dropping tables helps eliminate temporary or obsolete data structures. Careful planning is needed for both processes, including ensuring backups are available, assessing the effect on reliant applications, and maintaining active connections. Adopting version control procedures for database schemas, utilizing automated tools, and putting safety measures in place can all assist in reducing the dangers connected to these potent activities. A clean, dependable, and efficient database environment depends on properly controlling these processes.

CHAPTER VII

Database Security and User Management

User Roles and Permissions

The core components of database security and administration are user roles and permissions. They specify who has access to the database, what they may do, and how the security and integrity of the data are preserved. Database administrators (DBAs) must create, manage, and revoke permissions for users to protect sensitive data from illegal access and guarantee that the proper people have the right degrees of access.

Establishing accounts that permit people or programs to communicate with the database is the first step in creating and maintaining users in a database. Usually, this process starts with the DBA executing SQL instructions to create a user account. For example, the command may seem like this: `CREATE USER 'username'@'hostname' IDENTIFIED BY 'password';` in many SQL-based systems. With the given username, host from which the user can connect, and password for authentication, this program creates a new user. To improve security, the DBA can set up different properties, including password policies, account lockout policies, and expiration dates once the user has been created. To ensure that only active users have access, proper user management involves routinely monitoring user accounts and deactivating or removing those no longer needed.

One crucial step in determining what actions a user can conduct within the database is permitting them. Privileges, sometimes called permissions, can be used for various functions, from simple read-and-write operations to more complex ones like managing other users or building and altering database structures. Users are granted these permissions through the GRANT statement. For instance, the command `GRANT SELECT ON employees TO 'Alice';` might be used to allow a user called 'Alice' access SELECT data from a table called 'employees.' Granted at many levels, including global, database, table, and column levels, permissions provide more precise management of user capabilities. For example, restricting a user's access to a table's columns guarantees that sensitive data can be viewed without jeopardizing the dataset as a whole.

Removing previously granted permissions from a user is known as revocation of permissions. To accomplish this, the REVOKE statement is used. For instance, the command `REVOKE SELECT ON employees FROM 'Alice';` might be used to revoke the SELECT permission from 'Alice' on the 'employees' table. To minimize security risks and ensure that users no longer have access to database resources they no longer need, rescinding permissions is just as important as issuing them. User permissions should be regularly audited to help find and remove unused or excessive privileges that can be a security risk.

By consolidating a range of privileges granted to users, user roles provide a productive means of managing permissions. A DBA can construct roles with predetermined rights and assign these roles to users rather than giving each user unique access. This method makes administration of user permissions easier, particularly in large businesses with many users. For example, SELECT permissions on multiple tables could be granted to a role called "read_only," which would then be allocated to any user. `CREATE ROLE read_only;` and `GRANT SELECT ON employees TO read_only;}` could be the syntax for establishing a role. Next, the role is issued to users using `GRANT read_only TO 'alice';}`. This guarantees uniformity across users with comparable access requirements and streamlines permission management.

Maintaining the efficacy and efficiency of database operations is just as important as maintaining security when managing users and permissions. For instance, a DBA can stop malicious or accidental data updates by restricting rights to the minimum required for users to carry out their duties. According to the principle of least privilege, users should only be granted the lowest amount of access (or rights) necessary to carry out their duties. By doing this, the attack surface and possible harm from hacked accounts are decreased.

Advanced features like role hierarchies, which allow roles to inherit permissions from other roles, and context-sensitive permissions, which enable access based on query context like the user's location or time of day, are frequently supported by database systems for managing users and permissions. DBAs can customize access controls to satisfy intricate organizational requirements thanks to these features, which provide further flexibility and protection layers.

Effective administration of users and permissions includes procedural and policy elements and technical controls. Clear policies about user access to databases, together with protocols for requesting, approving, and reviewing access, should be established by organizations. Users are guaranteed to comprehend the significance of data security and their role in preserving it through regular training and awareness campaigns. To ensure that policies are followed, and access controls are still in place, periodic audits and compliance checks are helpful.

Managing user roles and permissions requires both auditing and monitoring. Monitoring user activity within the database is part of auditing, which helps identify and address unauthorized activity. This can involve keeping track of user account modifications, successful and unsuccessful login attempts, and actions taken with sensitive data. Real-time notifications for questionable activity, such as unauthorized access or unauthorized changes to vital data, can be obtained using monitoring systems. DBAs can maintain the security of the database environment by promptly identifying and mitigating security problems by combining auditing and monitoring with automated technologies.

Moreover, identity and access management (IAM) solutions can improve security and simplify administration by integrating user and permission management. IAM systems make single sign-on (SSO) and multi-factor authentication possible, which offer centralized management of user identities (MFA). Organizations can simplify the management of user accounts and permissions and enforce uniform access controls throughout all systems by connecting database access to an IAM system.

In conclusion, crucial database administration responsibilities that guarantee data security and operational effectiveness include generating, managing, and rescinding user permissions. To streamline and standardize access management, the procedure entails creating user accounts, granting and removing rights, and utilizing roles. Security is improved by integrating with IAM systems, applying sophisticated permission capabilities, and abiding by the least privilege principle. Access controls are kept efficient and adaptable to the company's demands through routine audits, monitoring, and policy adherence. DBAs can safeguard confidential information, uphold data integrity, and guarantee that the database environment effectively and securely satisfies the company's operational needs by carefully monitoring user roles and permissions.

Securing Data

Data security is of utmost importance in the current digital environment, where risks to data confidentiality and integrity are constant. Robust backup and recovery plans and data encryption are two essential elements of data security. When combined, these procedures guarantee data availability, shield data from unwanted access, and ease recovery in the case of data loss or corruption.

Data encryption employs cryptographic techniques to change readable data, or plaintext, into an unreadable one, or ciphertext. This conversion ensures the original data is only accessible to those who are allowed and have the correct decryption key. Data at rest, information kept on tangible media like hard drives, databases, and backups, and data in transit, or information moved over networks, can benefit from encryption.

Different encryption algorithms exist, each with varying performance and security properties. The same key is used for encryption and decryption in symmetric encryption techniques, including Advanced Encryption Standard (AES). These algorithms work well for encrypting considerable amounts of data and are typically faster. A public key is used for encryption, and a private key is used for decryption in asymmetric encryption techniques like RSA. Asymmetric algorithms are generally slower and less suitable for bulk data encryption, even when they are more secure for specific applications like digital signatures and key exchange.

Data encryption requires a few different stages to implement. Organizations must first determine which data, in light of sensitivity and legal restrictions, has to be encrypted. For example, the law frequently requires financial documents, health records, and personally identifiable information (PII) to be encrypted. They must next select suitable essential management procedures and encryption techniques. Since the protection and lifecycle management of encryption keys play a significant role in the security of encrypted data, effective key management is essential. This entails creating robust keys, keeping them safe, rotating them regularly, and revoking them when needed.

Since encrypted data can still be lost or distorted, encryption is not a cure-all for data security. As a result, putting strong backup and recovery procedures in place is equally crucial. Making copies of data is a critical component of backup systems since they enable data restoration in the event of data loss incidents such as hardware malfunctions, unintentional deletions, cyberattacks, or natural catastrophes. Recovery plans specify how to restore data from backups and guarantee minimally disruptive business operations.

Backups come in three varieties: differential, incremental, and complete. A full backup creates a comprehensive snapshot by duplicating all the data at one point, but it takes a lot of time and storage space. Multiple incremental backups may need to be applied, which could complicate the recovery process. Incremental backups are faster and require less storage since they only replicate the data that has changed since the last backup. Differential backups compromise between full and incremental backups regarding speed and storage needs by copying data that has changed since the previous full backup.

These many backup formats are usually combined in a well-thought-out backup strategy to balance recovery time objectives (RTOs), backup speed, and storage efficiency. An enterprise could run differential backups midweek, daily incremental backups, and weekly full backups. This strategy minimizes storage requirements and backup window durations while guaranteeing that data may be promptly restored from the most recent backups.

The selection of backup storage media and locations is critical to backup methods. Conventional choices include local disaster-prone on-site storage systems like external hard drives and cassettes, which provide rapid access but could be more reliable. Off-site backups offer more protection against local disruptions because they are kept in remote locations or on cloud storage. Still, they may also come with more excellent prices and longer recovery times. Many firms employ a hybrid method that combines off-site and on-site backups to balance speed, affordability, and security.

Cloud-based backup solutions have become increasingly popular because of their increased security features, scalability, and ease of management. Automated backup scheduling, data encryption both in transit and at rest, and interaction with disaster recovery as a service (DRaaS) solutions—which provide extensive recovery choices in the event of severe incidents—are standard features of these services. Organizations should consider data sovereignty concerns, regulatory compliance, and the security and dependability of the cloud backup service when selecting one.

A successful strategy must include testing backup and recovery techniques; this is a crucial but frequently disregarded step. Testing regularly guarantees that backups are operating as intended and that data can be restored reasonably. Testing might reveal problems like damaged backup files, inadequate storage, or incorrect backup schedule configurations. Additionally, it facilitates staff familiarization with recovery protocols, which lowers response times and mistakes in real-world recovery events.

The 3-2-1 rule states that you should save at least three copies of your data, store two copies on various media types, and keep one copy off-site, another crucial factor to consider when backing up and recovering data. After a data loss event, this rule offers a high degree of redundancy and raises the likelihood of successful data recovery.

Enterprises should implement comprehensive data security policies and practices in addition to encryption and backup plans. These include staff training initiatives, network security measures, access limits, and routine security audits. The risk of internal threats is reduced when only authorized workers can access sensitive data. At the same time, network security measures like firewalls, intrusion detection systems, and secure communication protocols mitigate the risk of external attacks. Regular training and awareness initiatives update employees on the newest security threats and data security best practices.

Various legal and regulatory standards must also be met via data encryption and backup plans. A few examples of industry- and region-specific data protection laws are the Payment Card Industry Data Security Standard (PCI DSS), the Health Insurance Portability and Accountability Act (HIPAA) in the US, and the General Data Protection Regulation (GDPR) in the EU. Adherence to these regulations mitigates legal ramifications and improves the organization's overall security stance.

It is imperative to secure data using encryption and effective backup and recovery procedures to prevent data breaches, loss, and corruption. Effective key management procedures are essential for preserving the security of encrypted data, which is transformed into an unreadable format to guarantee access only by authorized users in the event of a loss; backup and recovery techniques that include frequent backups, a variety of storage media, and extensive testing guarantee that data may be promptly and precisely restored. When combined, these procedures provide a thorough approach to data security that aids in protecting confidential data, preserving business continuity, and regulatory compliance for enterprises.

Auditing and Monitoring

Database administration requires auditing and monitoring to guarantee data security, performance, and integrity. These procedures entail keeping track of modifications and database access and monitoring the system's operation to identify and address problems quickly. Organizations may defend against illegal access, enhance database operations, and ensure regulatory compliance by enforcing robust auditing and monitoring procedures.

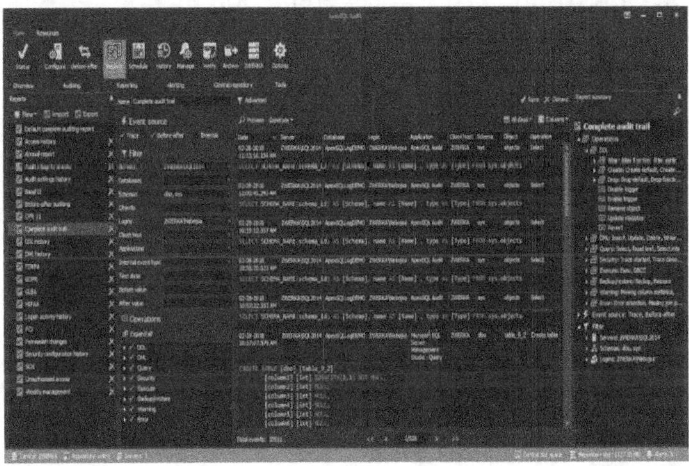

Tracking and documenting particular actions and events within the database is the purpose of auditing in the context of database management. This covers data alterations, schema adjustments, and attempted access. The main objective of auditing is to have an accurate record of who did what, when, and where. These logs are essential for maintaining an overall secure environment, guaranteeing compliance with numerous standards, and conducting forensic investigations in case of a security breach.

The following kinds of activities are usually tracked as part of a thorough auditing strategy: access to sensitive data, login, and logout activities, permission changes, data alterations (like INSERT, UPDATE, and DELETE operations), schema changes (like ALTER TABLE and CREATE INDEX). Organizations can create a transparent audit trail that aids in identifying possible security incidents and operational irregularities by recording these activities.

Database administrators (DBAs) can use features that most database management systems (DBMS) provide with built-in to implement audits. For instance, the Unified Auditing feature in Oracle Database simplifies the management and analysis of audit data by combining audit information from several sources into a single location. Similarly, SQL Server Audit from Microsoft SQL Server enables DBAs to create audit standards for monitoring events at the server and database levels. These systems usually allow for customizing recorded activities, guaranteeing thorough and effective audits.

Monitoring database access is yet another essential auditing component. Monitoring database access entails maintaining tabs on who logs in, what information they obtain, and how frequently. This ensures that users only access the data required for their tasks and helps detect attempts at illegal access. It also helps identify potential insider threats. Sophisticated monitoring solutions can send out real-time notifications in case of suspicious activity, such as many unsuccessful login attempts or access to sensitive data after regular work hours.

A robust and effective database infrastructure depends on regular performance monitoring and security-focused auditing. Monitoring performance entails keeping track of several database operation-related variables, including query response times, transaction rates, CPU and memory utilization, disk input/output, and network latency. By regularly monitoring these indicators, DBAs can spot and fix performance bottlenecks before they affect users or applications.

Database performance monitoring tools like Oracle Enterprise Manager, SQL Server Management Studio, and third-party programs like SolarWinds Database Performance Analyzer and Dynatrace offer comprehensive insights into the health and performance of databases. Typical features of these technologies include warning systems, historical data analysis, real-time dashboards, and automated performance adjustment recommendations.

Finding and improving slow-running queries is a crucial component of performance monitoring. Poorly could be better crafted, or more efficient queries can drastically reduce database performance, resulting in resource consumption and delayed response times. DBAs can increase speed by adding indexes, rewriting queries, or modifying database configuration settings by examining query execution plans and finding troublesome queries.

Resource management is a crucial component of performance monitoring. System resources such as CPU, memory, disk space, and network bandwidth are all consumed by databases. Monitoring resource usage enables you to ensure that resources are being used effectively and that the database functions within reasonable bounds. For example, excessive disk I/O may indicate the need for hardware improvements or adjustments to data storage strategies. In contrast, high CPU utilization may indicate the need for query optimization or extra indexing.

Monitoring database availability and uptime is another important aspect of effective monitoring. Ensuring high availability is essential for many applications, especially those that provide functions vital to the business. Metrics like downtime, failover occurrences, and replication status can be tracked by monitoring tools to ensure the database is available when needed and that problems are immediately found and fixed.

Proactive monitoring can also assist in capacity planning. DBAs can estimate future demands and arrange for necessary upgrades or scaling measures by evaluating patterns in resource utilization and performance indicators. This keeps the database capable of handling growing workloads over time and helps minimize performance degradation brought on by a lack of resources.

Regulation adherence is yet another important factor that motivates audits and monitoring. To secure sensitive data and guarantee accountability, regulations like the Sarbanes-Oxley Act (SOX), the General Data Protection Regulation (GDPR), and the Health Insurance Portability and Accountability Act (HIPAA) need particular controls and auditing procedures. Organizations can demonstrate compliance with these rules, avoid legal repercussions, and improve their overall security posture by implementing robust auditing and monitoring procedures.

Besides conventional on-premises databases, comprehensive audits and monitoring are also necessary for cloud-based databases. Database activity tracking and analysis solutions are usually integrated into cloud providers' offerings. For tracking API requests and database operations, for instance, Google Cloud SQL provides Cloud Audit Logs, whereas Amazon RDS has capabilities like Enhanced Monitoring and CloudTrail. Utilizing these technologies guarantees cloud databases are as safe and effective as their on-premises equivalents.

Establishing explicit policies and processes is necessary for firms to manage audits and monitoring efficiently. This includes deciding which tasks need to be audited, putting suitable technologies for monitoring and alarms in place, and routinely reviewing audit logs and performance indicators. Furthermore, consistent training and awareness initiatives guarantee that DBAs and other pertinent staff members comprehend the significance of auditing and monitoring and are adept at utilizing the required instruments and methodologies.

To sum up, monitoring and auditing are crucial procedures for preserving databases' security, consistency, and functionality. During an audit, modifications and database access are monitored, and a thorough record of all activities is kept that can be utilized for security, compliance, and forensic analysis. Monitoring is concerned with measuring performance indicators, locating bottlenecks, and ensuring the database operates at peak efficiency. When combined, these procedures assist businesses in preventing unwanted access, quickly identifying and resolving problems, and guaranteeing the reliable and efficient operation of databases. Organizations may fulfill their operational and regulatory obligations while maintaining a secure and efficient database environment by implementing robust auditing and monitoring methods.

CHAPTER VIII

Transactions and Concurrency Control

Understanding Transactions

Database management requires a fundamental understanding of transactions because it guarantees data consistency and integrity despite concurrent processes or system failures. The foundation of transaction processing in relational databases is the ACID characteristics (Atomicity, Consistency, Isolation, and Durability). These characteristics guarantee that, despite several difficulties, transactions are handled consistently, and the database is kept up to date. The SQL statements BEGIN, COMMIT, and ROLLBACK, which regulate the beginning, ending, and reversal of transactions, are essential to transaction management.

The idea that a transaction is an indivisible unit of work is known as atomicity. This indicates that either every operation in a transaction is successfully finished or none is. Partial transactions won't cause the database to become inconsistent because of atomicity. When money is transferred between accounts in a financial system, for instance, one account must be debited, and another must be credited. Money cannot be debited without a matching credit because atomicity ensures that either operations happen or neither happens.

When a transaction moves the database from one legitimate state to another while abiding by all established guidelines and limitations, consistency guarantees this. This characteristic preserves database integrity by ensuring that all data written to the database complies with all established policies, including foreign keys, unique constraints, and other relational integrity constraints. For example, a transaction that violates a database rule prohibiting a negative account balance would be rolled back to maintain consistency.

The visibility of transaction updates to other concurrent transactions is determined by isolation. It ensures that intermediate transaction states are hidden from other transactions until a transaction is finished. This avoids issues resulting in inconsistent data views as unclean, non-repeatable, and phantom reads. Different isolation levels offer varying degrees of isolation and performance trade-offs, including Read Uncommitted, Read Committed, Repeatable Read, and Serializable. High isolation levels, such as Serializable, avoid most concurrent problems. However, additional locking may hurt performance.

Durability ensures that, even in the case of a system failure, changes made to a transaction are irreversible once they are committed. Usually, publishing transaction logs to a disk or other reliable storage ensures this characteristic. The database can retrieve committed transactions from the logs in the case of a crash, guaranteeing that no data is lost. Applications where data permanence is essential, such as financial transactions, where losing transaction records could have dire repercussions, require durability.

The SQL commands BEGIN, COMMIT, and ROLLBACK is necessary to handle transactions. A new transaction is started by executing the BEGIN statement, which indicates the beginning of the transaction. Until a COMMIT or ROLLBACK statement is performed, all actions that come after are a part of this transaction. In a banking application, for instance, BEGIN might initiate a transaction that updates several accounts as a single logical unit of work.

A transaction is completed, and all modifications are irreversible with the COMMIT declaration. The database ensures all operations are applied and the changes are permanent when a transaction is committed. This implies that following a COMMIT, a transaction's consequences are apparent to other transactions and will endure even during a system failure. Using the banking example, a COMMIT would guarantee that the debits and credits are permanently recorded after the money transfer processes are finished.

On the other hand, the ROLLBACK statement cancels a transaction and reverses all of the actions that have been taken since the transaction started. This is essential to preserving integrity and consistency if a transaction has mistaken or problems. To ensure that no incomplete updates are left in the database, a ROLLBACK would, for example, reverse all changes made during an error when moving money between accounts. Preventing incorrect or incomplete transactions from being applied preserves the integrity of account balances.

In multi-user systems, transactions and the SQL statements used to handle them are essential for dependability and performance, in addition to maintaining consistency and integrity. Effective transaction management keeps users from interfering with one another's work in systems with several concurrent users, preventing data corruption and guaranteeing smooth functioning. Transactions, for instance, guarantee correct inventory counts in e-commerce applications, even when many users make simultaneous purchases of the same item.

Database administrators and developers must comprehend and put into practice ACID properties and transaction management techniques. The database and its transaction mechanisms must be carefully planned and configured to provide atomicity, consistency, isolation, and durability. According to the application's needs, this entails determining the necessary isolation levels, creating reliable transaction processing code that appropriately leverages BEGIN, COMMIT, and ROLLBACK, and implementing thorough logging and recovery procedures to guarantee durability.

Furthermore, many database management systems (DBMS) might provide further functionality or transaction management efficiencies. Savepoints, for example, let transactions be partially rolled back to a particular point without terminating the transaction entirely. This is made possible by certain DBMS. This can be helpful when several independent operations are carried out in complex transactions, and a partial rollback is necessary due to specific problems.

Distributed transaction management is required in distributed database setups because transactions may span several databases or systems. Coordinating several separate databases to ensure a transaction is committed across all systems involved or wholly rolled back is known as distributed transactions. Usually, techniques like the two-phase commit protocol (2PC), which guarantees atomicity and consistency across distributed systems, are used to manage this.

Understanding transactions is crucial for more reasons than technical ones; it significantly affects user experiences and corporate operations. For example, trustworthy transaction management is essential for healthcare systems, financial institutions, e-commerce sites, and any other application where data consistency and integrity directly impact consumer trust and service dependability. Protecting the organization's data and reputation involves ensuring that transactions are handled appropriately, and that the database complies with ACID properties. These measures also help to prevent errors, fraud, and data damage.

To sum up, proficient database management requires a comprehension of transactions, including the ACID features and the application of BEGIN, COMMIT, and ROLLBACK statements. Despite concurrent processes and system failures, these ideas guarantee transaction processing dependability while preserving data consistency and integrity. Database administrators and programmers may design dependable and secure applications with atomicity, consistency, isolation, and durability. Ensuring seamless multi-user operations, safeguarding data, and supporting essential business processes across diverse industries are all made possible by appropriately executing and managing transactions.

Isolation Levels and Locking

In database management, isolation levels, and locking methods are critical ideas necessary to preserve data consistency and integrity, especially in settings where multiple transactions co-occur. By controlling how transactions communicate with one another, these procedures guarantee dependable database operations and reduce anomalies. For database administrators and developers looking to maximize performance while maintaining data integrity, understanding the many types of locks, such as shared and exclusive, and the isolation levels—READ UNCOMMITTED, READ COMMITTED, REPEATABLE READ, and SERIALIZABLE—is essential.

The isolation levels determine the degree to which the operations in one transaction are isolated from those in other concurrent transactions. Data that has been updated by previous transactions but has not yet been committed can be viewed by a transaction using the least restrictive isolation level, viewed UNCOMMITTED. A transaction reading uncommitted data from another transaction is known as a "dirty read," which might result in several phenomena. This isolation level is rarely utilized in applications requiring excellent data correctness, even though it avoids many locks and delivers good performance at the expense of data abnormalities.

A transaction can only read data committed by other transactions with the more stringent READ COMMITTED isolation level than READ UNCOMMITTED. As a result, there are fewer dirty reads and a more consistent data view. It does not stop non-repeatable reads, which occur when a transaction reads the same data several times and discovers different values each time due to modifications made to the data by other transactions that committed those changes in between readings. READ COMMITTED is frequently utilized because it balances system efficiency and data consistency.

By guaranteeing that once a transaction reads data, another transaction cannot modify it until the initial transaction has finished, the REPEATABLE READ isolation level further limits concurrent transactions. As a result, there are fewer dirty and non-repeatable reads, increasing the consistency of the data. It does not stop phantom reads, which occur when a transaction reads a set of rows that meet a condition. Still, a subsequent transaction modifies or removes rows that meet the requirement, returning a different set of rows on future reads. Although REPEATABLE READ offers greater consistency than READ COMMITTED, its enhanced locking may hurt performance.

The strictest isolation level, SERIALIZABLE, guarantees total separation from other transactions. It prevents dirty, non-repeatable, and phantom reads by ensuring that transactions are carried out sequentially as if conducted one after the other. Although this level offers maximum consistency, it can substantially negatively affect performance because of frequent locking and the possibility of more transaction contention. Despite some performance penalties, SERIALIZABLE is utilized when data integrity is critical, such as financial applications.

Database management systems use locking methods to control concurrent access to data and impose isolation levels. A lock is a mechanism that prevents one transaction from accessing or changing a data item while another tries to access or modify it. Shared locks and exclusive locks are two general categories for locks. Shared locks let several transactions view the same data item at the same time, but they stop any one transaction from changing the data. When a transaction has to read data while preventing concurrent alterations, this lock is used to ensure the data is consistent during the read operation.

Conversely, exclusive locks stop other transactions from accessing or changing the data item. When a transaction wants to change data, it uses this form of lock to ensure that no other transaction can read or write to the data until the exclusive lock is released. Exclusive locks offer strong consistency guarantees but can also cause conflict and lower concurrency, particularly in systems with a large transaction volume.

Database management systems use different tactics to maximize performance, eliminate contention, and manage locks. One popular method is lock escalation, in which the system first locks individual pages or rows. Still, if the number of locks exceeds a predetermined threshold, it locks the entire database. Although handling several fine-grained locks is lessened, there may be more contention and less concurrency.

Deadlock detection and resolution is another tactic. When two or more transactions wait for one another to release locks, a cycle of dependencies that cannot be broken occurs, leading to deadlocks. Database systems usually employ algorithms to identify and break deadlocks, allowing the remaining transactions to continue once one or more implicated transactions are canceled. This guarantees the system can break out of deadlocks and sustain throughput.

The locking system and isolation level selection significantly impact database consistency and performance. Higher performance and concurrency are typically achieved with lower isolation levels and fewer locks, but there is a greater chance of data abnormalities. Higher isolation levels and more locks provide stronger consistency guarantees, but these measures might also lower performance because of increasing contention and locking costs. Database managers have to carefully weigh these trade-offs in light of the particular needs of their applications.

Since the READ COMMITTED isolation level offers a respectable trade-off between consistency and performance for many applications, many databases default. Nevertheless, despite their performance implications, higher isolation levels like REPEATABLE READ or SERIALIZABLE may be required for applications with strict consistency requirements, such as financial systems. On the other hand, applications that value speed above all else and have a low threshold for data abnormalities could go for less restrictive isolation settings, such as READ UNCOMMITTED.

Modern database systems frequently use different concurrency control strategies, such as multi-version concurrency control (MVCC) and optimistic concurrency control (ACC), in addition to conventional locking mechanisms. Optimistic concurrency control checks for conflicts solely at commit time, allowing transactions to proceed without first obtaining locks. Lowering lock contention can increase performance, but it calls on systems to identify and settle conflicts as soon as they arise.

Another cutting-edge method called MVCC keeps several copies of data items and lets transactions access various versions according to when they start. High concurrency is achieved with this method, which also stays clear of many of the drawbacks of conventional locking techniques. For example, because transactions can read previous versions of the data while others modify the current version, MVCC can guarantee consistent readings without locking. Databases like PostgreSQL and MySQL's InnoDB storage engine employ this strategy, which combines consistency and performance.

In conclusion, locking methods and isolation levels are essential to preserving data consistency and integrity in database systems, mainly where multiple transactions co-occur. Optimizing database performance while maintaining data integrity requires an understanding of the trade-offs between various isolation levels, such as READ UNCOMMITTED, READ COMMITTED, REPEATABLE READ, and SERIALIZABLE, as well as the implementation of suitable locking mechanisms, such as shared and exclusive locks. Database administrators have to balance the requirements for concurrency, performance, and consistency while carefully selecting and configuring these mechanisms based on the particular requirements of their applications. Sophisticated methods such as multi-version and optimistic concurrency control provide more approaches to concurrency management and enhance system efficiency, emphasizing the intricacy and significance of efficient transaction management in contemporary database systems.

Handling Deadlocks

Handling deadlocks is a crucial component of database administration that guarantees the seamless running of transactions in a multi-user setting. When two or more transactions wait for one another to release locks, a cycle of dependencies prevents the affected transactions from moving further, resulting in deadlocks. Database reliability and performance depend on knowing what causes deadlocks and applying effective deadlock detection and resolution techniques.

Resource contention is the leading cause of deadlocks in a multi-user database system. Multiple transactions may obtain locks on distinct resources in an order that results in a cyclic wait state when they compete for the same resources, such as data rows, tables, or other objects. Two transactions, for instance, can be considered: Transaction A locks Resource 1 and awaits Resource 2, whereas Transaction B locks Resource 2 and awaits Resource 1. There is a deadlock since neither transaction can move forward. Databases typically experience this scenario when transactions hold locks for extended periods and frequently use shared resources.

Deadlocks can arise due to several circumstances. Inadequate transaction architecture, which results in transactions locking resources in an irregular order, is one frequent cause. Deadlocks are more likely to occur when multiple transactions obtain locks on the same set of resources but in distinct sequences. Long-running transactions that retain locks for extended periods are another element that increases the likelihood of contention for other transactions. The possibility of deadlocks is also increased by high concurrency and intense read-write operations since multiple transactions compete for resources simultaneously.

Finding deadlocks in a system is known as deadlock detection. Different approaches are used by database management systems (DBMS) to identify deadlocks. A popular technique is the wait-for graph. Using this method, the DBMS creates a graph in which each node represents a transaction, and the directed edges show the relationships between pending transactions. A stalemate exists if a cycle is seen in the wait-for graph. This approach is practical in quickly identifying deadlocks so the system can take corrective action.

Timeout-based detection is an additional strategy for deadlock detection. The DBMS uses this technique to track how long transactions wait for locks. The system senses a deadlock and initiates action to break it if a transaction takes longer than the predetermined wait time. Although this approach is more straightforward to put into practice, it could cause false positives, ending transactions that are only experiencing higher wait times rather than being in a deadlock.

Stalemate resolution is the following action to take after a stalemate is identified. Resolving deadlocks primarily aims to break the circle of dependence so that transactions can continue. Transaction rollback is a popular tactic in which one or more stalled transactions are aborted and rolled back to their initial state. As a result, the resources used by the canceled transactions are released, enabling the ongoing transactions to proceed. Usually, factors including transaction age, priority, and resource use are considered when deciding which transactions to roll back. To reduce the impact on the system, the DBMS may roll back the transaction that has done the most minor work.

Preemptive resource allocation is another technique for resolving deadlocks. In this method, the DBMS gives the waiting transactions the resources they need to break the impasse temporarily. This strategy may only sometimes be practical and can be more challenging to apply, mainly if it causes other transactions to starve for resources.

One essential component of database management is detection, resolution, and deadlock prevention. Lock ordering is one preventive method where the DBMS maintains a consistent order in which transactions obtain locks on resources. There is less chance of cyclic wait situations when transactions adhere to the same lock acquisition sequence. Another protective strategy is locking timeout settings, automatically releasing locks if a transaction cannot acquire all required resources in the allotted period. This lessens the possibility of protracted lines and other bottlenecks.

Preventing deadlocks also requires optimal transaction architecture. Developers should minimize the time that locks are held by keeping transactions brief and to the point. Lowering the scope of locked resources and avoiding needless locks can lessen the likelihood of disputes. Locking just the rows a transaction needs to access rather than the entire table might significantly lower the possibility of deadlocks.

Another proactive tactic is deadlock avoidance, in which the DBMS dynamically assesses transaction requests and only issues locks in cases where they do not raise the possibility of a stalemate. Deadlock avoidance strategies like the wound-wait and wait-die techniques are frequently employed. A younger transaction is preempted and rolled back (wounded) in the wound-wait technique if an older transaction requests a lock held by the latter. The younger transaction waits if it seeks a lock that is being held by the older transaction. An older transaction in the wait-die scheme waits if it demands a lock held by a younger transaction. A transaction is rolled back (dies) if it requires a lock held by a previous transaction. These methods prevent deadlocks by guaranteeing that transactions are either allowed to continue or terminated before a deadlock can occur.

Deadlocks can be efficiently managed by continuously assessing and optimizing database performance. Regularly examining transaction patterns, database logs, and system performance metrics can assist in identifying deadlock-prone locations. DBAs can then apply well-informed modifications to resource management policies, isolation levels, and transaction logic to reduce the likelihood of deadlock.

The management of deadlocks also requires awareness and training. Expertise in transaction management best practices and the particular characteristics and actions of the database management system (DBMS) they are utilizing is essential for database administrators and developers. Teams may create more reliable and effective systems by better understanding how various isolation levels, locking techniques, and transaction patterns affect the occurrence of deadlocks.

To summarize, managing deadlocks entails comprehending their origins, implementing efficient detection and resolution techniques, and applying preventative actions to reduce their frequency. In multi-user contexts, resource congestion leads to deadlocks, which various reasons, including transaction design, concurrency levels, and lock duration can cause. Deadlock resolution usually entails transaction rollback or preemptive resource allocation, while deadlock detection can be accomplished with tools such as wait-for graphs and timeout-based approaches. Preventive techniques significantly decrease deadlock hazards, including lock ordering, lock timeout settings, and efficient transaction architecture. Database administrators and developers can ensure smooth and efficient transaction processing by maintaining high levels of performance and reliability in their systems by integrating detection, resolution, and prevention strategies.

CHAPTER IX

Performance Tuning and Optimization

Indexing Strategies

In database management, indexing strategies are essential for improving the effectiveness and speed of data retrieval. A data structure called an index increases the speed at which data can be retrieved from a database table, but it also requires more storage space and time to insert and update data. The efficiency of indexes stems from their capacity to reduce the volume of data scanned during SELECT, UPDATE, and DELETE statement operations, optimizing query performance. The proper index form must be chosen for a given scenario because there are several indexes, each with unique characteristics and use cases.

One of the most basic types of indexing is the main index. It is usually created on a table's primary key. The primary index guarantees speedy access to records based on the primary key since primary keys are distinct and non-null. This kind of index is created automatically on tables with primary critical constraints declared. The key to primary indexes' effectiveness is their capacity to arrange data sequentially; they frequently utilize B-tree structures, which speed up lookup, insertion, and deletion processes.

Non-clustered or secondary indexes offer an effective way to retrieve data depending on fields other than the primary key. When queries routinely filter or sort data based on columns other than the primary key, these indexes are useful. Unlike primary indexes, secondary indexes do not control the data's actual storage order. Instead, they uphold an independent framework that refers to the exact locations of the data rows. While there may be overhead associated with this extra structure, for specific access patterns, query efficiency is much enhanced.

The actual order of the data in a table is determined by clustered indexes, which makes them unique. A table's rows are stored on disk according to the order of the indexed column(s) when a clustered index is formed. With sequential data storage, this index is quite effective for range-based queries. However, a table can only have one clustered index because it determines the actual physical storage order. Clustered indexes are commonly used in range queries and are best suited for highly unique columns.

In contrast, non-clustered indexes do not affect the data's storage order. Alternatively, they produce a different data structure with a sorted list of references to the actual data. Any column, including ones currently a part of a clustered index, can be the basis for a non-clustered index. They help queries that filter, sort, or connect tables based on columns other than the primary key execute better.

Indexing multiple columns together creates composite indexes, also called multi-column indexes. When queries frequently filter or sort data based on combinations of columns, these indexes come in handy. A composite index's column arrangement is essential since it influences its performance. For instance, an index on columns (A, B) can effectively manage queries that filter on A just or A and B together but not on B alone. Composite indexes can significantly improve performance, but they must be carefully constructed to meet the query patterns.

By guaranteeing no duplicate values, unique indexes enforce the uniqueness of the indexed columns. When columns are defined with unique constraints, these indexes are automatically generated. Unique indexes are very helpful for columns that should have unique values, like email addresses or social security numbers. Unique indexes guarantee data integrity and enhance query performance by enabling quick lookups for unique values.

Specialized indexes used for text-based searches are called full-text indexes. Large text fields and sophisticated search queries, including those incorporating phrases, proximity, and weighting, are supported by their architecture. Full-text indexes rapidly find rows containing particular words or phrases using algorithms such as inverted indexing. Applications like content management systems and search engines that demand sophisticated text search capabilities depend on these indexes.

Another specialized index type that is mainly utilized in data warehousing and environments with workloads that include a lot of reading is the bitmap index. When there are fewer unique values in a column than in rows, it is said to have low cardinality and, hence, be efficient. Binary vectors, or bitmaps, are used by bitmap indexes to indicate whether a particular value is present in a row. This indexing technique can significantly reduce the amount of storage space needed and enhance query performance for some kinds of queries, especially those that involve AND, OR, and NOT operations.

Effective index creation and use necessitate carefully evaluating the workload characteristics, query patterns, and database schema. Analyzing query performance using instruments like the query execution plan is one of the most important tactics. These tools assist in determining which queries are good candidates for indexing and which currently existing indexes are underutilized. To maximize performance and storage, opportunities for adding new indexes or removing unnecessary ones can be found through routine monitoring and analysis.

Another essential component of successful indexing strategies is index maintenance. Performance can suffer due to index fragmentation brought on by data alterations over time. Rebuilding or restructuring indexes are examples of regular index maintenance procedures that assist in preserving optimal performance. Furthermore, updating statistics about indexed columns guarantees correct data that the query optimizer can use to create effective execution plans.

Another critical aspect is balancing the number of indexes. Too many indexes might cause overhead during data update operations like INSERT, UPDATE, and DELETE, even though they can significantly increase query performance. Performance may be slowed down by the need to update all pertinent indexes after each modification operation. To avoid having too much influence on data modification processes, it is crucial to create indexes that maximize the advantage for the queries run most frequently.

To sum up, indexing strategies are essential to optimizing database speed. Database managers can significantly improve query performance by comprehending and utilizing the many index kinds, including primary, secondary, clustered, non-clustered, composite, unique, full-text, and bitmap. Analyzing query trends, carrying out routine maintenance, and adjusting the amount of indexes to attain peak performance are all necessary for effective indexing. Indexes can improve data retrieval performance by guaranteeing that the database can process complex queries and big datasets quickly and accurately with careful preparation and continuous monitoring.

Query Optimization

To improve the effectiveness and performance of database operations, query optimization is a crucial component of database management. It entails examining and improving queries to reduce resource use and execution time. The EXPLAIN plan, which offers insights into how a database management system (DBMS) performs a query, is one of the most valuable tools for query optimization. Database administrators and developers can detect bottlenecks and adopt ways to optimize queries, ensuring faster and more efficient data retrieval by comprehending and utilizing the EXPLAIN plan.

Analyzing the effectiveness of current queries is the first step in the query optimization process. This entails figuring out which queries are resource-hungry or slow. Using the EXPLAIN plan, a tool in most database management systems (DBMSs), is typically the first step. It provides information about the query optimizer's execution approach. The EXPLAIN plan deconstructs the query into its constituent pieces. It explains the order of operations, the indexes used, and the approximate cost of each operation that the DBMS plans to do for each section.

It is necessary to be familiar with each EXPLAIN plan's components to comprehend its result. The plan usually contains details on the tables that are part of the query, the join operations carried out, how indexes are used, and how many rows are expected to be processed at each stage. Essential parameters like selectivity, cardinality, and cost are also given. Cardinality is the estimated number of rows processed, whereas cost is the projected amount of resources used to execute the query. The percentage of rows filtered by a specific operation is called selectivity. These measurements can be used to identify areas that could use improvement and to pinpoint unproductive operations.

The lack of proper indexes is one common problem identified by the EXPLAIN plan. Because they minimize the number of rows scanned during query execution, indexes are essential for accelerating data retrieval. Performance can be significantly improved by placing an index on the required columns if the EXPLAIN plan reveals that a full table scan is being carried out. For instance, an index on a particular column can speed up a query by minimizing the need to read the entire table when it regularly filters data based on that column.

Another crucial area where the EXPLAIN plan offers insightful information is joins. When working with massive datasets, join procedures can be highly resource-intensive. The join—nested loop, hash, or merge join—and the sequence in which the tables are connected are disclosed in the EXPLAIN plan. Ensing the join columns are indexed, and the join order is suitable is a common step in optimizing join operations. There are times when substantial speed gains can be achieved by changing the query to take advantage of joins that are more effective or by dissecting complicated, joins into smaller, more manageable steps.

Rewriting queries is a frequent optimization technique. The performance of a query might occasionally be affected by how it is worded. The EXPLAIN plan has the ability to identify inefficiencies in the query structure, including excessive or repetitive subqueries. Improved performance can be achieved by reorganizing the query to use preexisting indexes or simplifying it by eliminating unnecessary actions. For example, utilizing set operations like UNION or INTERSECT or converting subqueries to joins can frequently lead to more effective execution strategies.

Query performance is affected by hardware resources and database configuration in addition to structural optimizations. The EXPLAIN plan can show whether memory or CPU resources constrain a particular operation. Optimizing the database settings in these situations, such as changing the cache sizes or allowing parallel processing, can be beneficial. Maintaining optimal query performance requires ensuring the database server has enough memory, CPU, and storage.

Another essential component of query optimization is keeping track of and maintaining statistics. The query optimizer looks to statistics regarding data distribution in tables and indexes to make wise selections. More accurate or updated statistics may result in less-than-ideal execution strategies. Updating statistics regularly guarantees that the optimizer has access to the most recent data, allowing it to select the execution strategy that will maximize efficiency. The EXPLAIN plan might highlight differences between estimated and actual row counts, signaling the necessity for statistics changes.

Sometimes, query optimization calls for more sophisticated methods, like materialized views or table splitting. Partitioning uses predetermined criteria, like date ranges, to split a massive table into smaller, easier-to-manage sections. This can drastically lower the quantity of data examined during queries—especially when dealing with big datasets. Conversely, materialized views can expedite repetitive, resource-intensive tasks by storing the outcomes of complex searches. The EXPLAIN plan can assist in identifying queries that may profit from these sophisticated methods by pointing up costly actions that could be made more efficient by materialized views or partitioning.

Lastly, query optimization is a continuous endeavor. Sustaining optimal performance requires ongoing monitoring and analysis as data quantities increase and query patterns change. Examining the EXPLAIN plans for frequently run queries can aid in finding new areas for improvement. Furthermore, keeping up with DBMS changes and new features might offer fresh methods and tools for enhancing query efficiency.

To sum up, query optimization is essential to effective database administration. Using the EXPLAIN plan to analyze and optimize queries offers profound insights into the DBMS's execution techniques. Database administrators and developers can find inefficiencies, apply indexing methods, rewrite queries, optimize join operations, and ensure that the database settings and statistics are current by comprehending the comprehensive information offered by the EXPLAIN plan. In addition to constant monitoring and analysis, sophisticated techniques like partitioning and materialized views guarantee that databases can process ever-increasing volumes of data and change query patterns quickly and effectively. Efficient query optimization yields faster and more responsive apps, increasing performance and improving user experience overall.

Database Maintenance

Managing and guaranteeing database systems' long-term functionality, dependability, and health requires regular database maintenance. Frequent maintenance duties encompass a variety of actions intended to maximize database efficiency, avert problems, and guarantee data accuracy. These chores include maintaining disk space, applying patches and updates, rearranging or rebuilding indexes, updating statistics, assessing performance indicators, and making backups. Database administrators (DBAs) can improve the effectiveness and stability of database operations by methodically completing these duties.

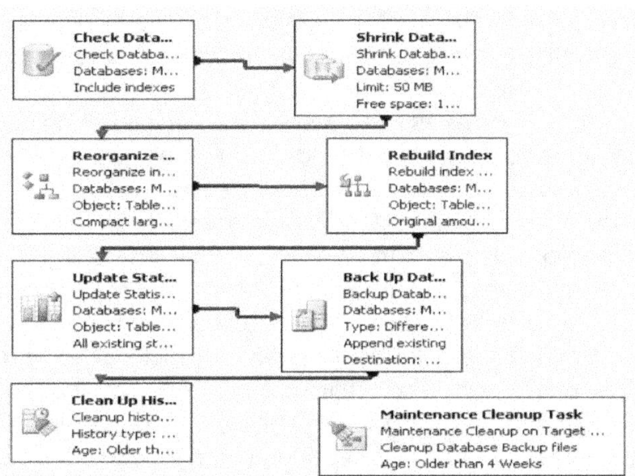

The routine study of performance indicators is one of the core components of database maintenance. This entails monitoring essential metrics, including disk I/O rates, CPU and memory consumption, and query execution times. In-depth insights into these metrics are provided by tools like database monitoring software and integrated DBMS features, which assist DBAs in locating performance bottlenecks and areas needing optimization. For example, persistently high disk input/output rates could indicate inefficient searches or improved indexing. DBAs can prevent user impact by proactively examining these indicators and addressing performance issues early.

Statistics updating is yet another essential upkeep duty. Database optimizers use statistics to help them decide on the best query execution strategies. These statistics cover the distribution of data in tables and indexes, including the number of rows, the distribution of critical values, and the selectivity of columns. These statistics may become outdated if new data is added, changed, or removed over time, which could result in less-than-ideal query strategies. Updating statistics regularly guarantees that the optimizer has up-to-date, correct data, which facilitates the creation of effective query execution plans.

Modern DBMSs frequently automate this procedure but should still be watched to ensure it functions properly.

Maintaining indexes is also crucial to maximizing database performance. Although indexes are essential for accelerating data retrieval, data insertions, updates, and deletions may cause them to fragment over time. Slower query performance and wasteful disk I/O might result from fragmented indexes. Index rebuilds and reorganizations regularly can reduce fragmentation. By rearranging the leaf-level pages in an index, reorganizing it defragments it and improves data retrieval speed without requiring a complete rebuild. On the other hand, rebuilding an index involves using more resources but results in a thorough index reconstruction, which can significantly increase performance. Rebuilding or reorganizing depends on the degree of fragmentation and the length of the available maintenance window.

Another essential component of database management is managing disk space. Databases use more disk space as they get larger, which can cause storage problems and affect performance. DBAs can guarantee adequate capacity for database operations by routinely monitoring disk use. This comprises transaction logs, backups, temporary files, and the main data files. Putting techniques like data archiving into practice—moving outdated and seldom used data to less expensive storage —can aid in efficient disk space management. Regular cleanup activities can also increase performance and free up significant disk space. Examples of these jobs include deleting unnecessary items and discarding outdated data.

Backup and recovery are essential parts of database management that guarantee the availability and preservation of data. Regular backups are vital to protect against data loss due to hardware malfunctions, software defects, or human mistakes. Depending on the recovery model and business needs of the database, DBAs need to implement a robust backup strategy that includes differential, complete, and transaction log backups. It is equally crucial to regularly test backups by executing restore operations to ensure they are reliable and functional during a disaster. Doing this allows backup procedure problems to be found and fixed before an actual need emerges.

Applying patches and upgrades is another crucial maintenance operation that keeps the database system safe and operating at peak efficiency. Database providers often provide updates and patches to address security flaws, correct errors, and improve performance. Maintaining the database's functionality and shielding it from security risks requires keeping up with these modifications. Implementing patches and upgrades necessitates meticulous preparation and testing to prevent interruptions to database operations. To guarantee the least possible impact on users, DBAs should have a well-defined procedure for assessing, testing, and deploying updates.

Maintaining security settings and user access are additional aspects of database maintenance. This involves routinely checking and updating user permissions to ensure that only individuals with authorization may access the database and its resources. Enabling encryption, employing solid passwords, and checking access logs are some examples of best practices for database security that may be implemented to help shield the database from potential breaches and unwanted access. The database can be kept safe by identifying and reducing possible security threats through routine security audits and vulnerability assessments.

Performance optimization is a crucial component of database maintenance. To maximize performance, this entails adjusting a variety of database setups and factors.

Database speed can be significantly impacted by, among other things, modifying memory allocation settings, setting up suitable cache sizes, and making the best use of temporary space. Based on the workload and usage patterns of the database, DBAs should periodically analyze and modify these parameters. In addition to rewriting wasteful queries, building suitable indexes, and utilizing the DBMS's speed-enhancing capabilities, performance tuning also entails optimizing queries.

DBAs should do routine maintenance and plan ahead for and oversee database expansion. This is capacity planning, in which projected business demands and current usage patterns are used to estimate future storage and performance requirements. DBAs may make sure that the database architecture is scalable and can handle increasing workloads without sacrificing performance by making growth plans. This could entail deploying database sharding or partitioning techniques, adding extra storage, or updating hardware.

Database maintenance is a complex, continuous activity necessary to provide the best possible performance, dependability, and security for database systems. Maintaining a healthy database environment requires regular maintenance tasks like managing disk space, applying patches and updates, reorganizing or rebuilding indexes, analyzing performance metrics, updating statistics, controlling user access, and optimizing performance. DBAs may avoid problems, maximize performance, and guarantee that databases can successfully serve the demands of the business by methodically carrying out these activities. Proactive and conscientious database maintenance ultimately results in increased effectiveness, decreased downtime, and improved data integrity—all of which are essential for any organization that depends on database systems to succeed.

CHAPTER X

Practical Applications and Advanced Topics

Working with Large Datasets

Managing enormous datasets is a critical difficulty in big data analytics and database management. Traditional database systems generally need help maintaining performance and scalability as data quantities expand dramatically. Partitioning and sharding are used to overcome these issues, enabling effective data management and enhanced query performance. These techniques are crucial for guaranteeing that databases can manage enormous volumes of data without sacrificing dependability or speed.

Using a process known as partitioning, a considerable dataset is divided into smaller, more manageable sections known as partitions. Each division comprises a subset of the data that may be handled and accessed separately. There are several criteria on which this split can be made, including range, list, hash, and composite approaches. Range partitioning is especially helpful for time-series data since searches frequently include precise date ranges. It partitions data based on a continuous range of values.

In contrast, list partitioning divides data according to pre-established lists of values and works well with categorically different datasets. By employing a hash function to divide data equally among partitions, hash partitioning ensures balanced workloads and keeps no single division from acting as a bottleneck. To further maximize efficiency, composite partitioning combines many partitioning techniques.

Partitioning has several benefits, mainly improved query performance and manageability. Queries can run more quickly when a large dataset is divided into smaller divisions since they frequently only need to scan the pertinent partitions rather than the whole dataset. Processing of queries is accelerated, and this selective scanning decreases I/O operations. Furthermore, partitioning makes these chores easier because maintenance operations like backup, restore, and index management may be carried out on particular partitions rather than the entire dataset. Because several partitions can be accessed concurrently without causing conflict, it also enhances the system's capacity to manage concurrent access.

Partitioning and sharding are closely related techniques that involve dividing data among several servers da, database instances, or shards. A portion of the total data is contained in each shard, which is a fully functional, separate database. Generally, sharding is used to do horizontal scaling, which enables a database to add extra servers to manage an increase in load. A shard key frequently dictates the data allocation to each shard in this distribution. Critical shard selection is essential to guarantee uniform data distribution and peak performance. It can be one or many columns.

Sharding has many advantages. Above all, it makes it possible to handle more enormous datasets by utilizing the combined power of several servers. This simultaneously boosts processing power and storage capacity, enabling quicker query processing and data manipulation. Sharding also increases availability and fault tolerance because the failure of one shard doesn't impact the others. Furthermore, it makes geographic distribution easier, allowing data to be kept closer to users and lowering latency for applications that are spread out geographically.

However, there are drawbacks to both partitioning and sharding that need to be considered appropriately. Partitioning effectively necessitates choosing the correct partition keys and keeping partition size and query performance in check. Excessive overhead may result from too little of a partition, while the advantages of partitioning may be defeated by too large of a partition. Similarly, to prevent hotspots and guarantee even load distribution, sharding requires meticulous preparation of the shard key and management of data dissemination. Other complications that need to be addressed are rebalancing shards, managing cross-shard queries, and preserving data consistency between shards.

In contemporary database systems, partitioning and sharding are crucial methods for handling massive datasets. Partitioning divides data into smaller, more manageable bits, which improves query performance and makes maintenance easier. In contrast, sharding increases capacity and fault tolerance by splitting data across several database servers to accomplish horizontal scaling. Both approaches necessitate meticulous planning and administration to maximize performance and guarantee the effective handling of extensive data. Organizations can leverage the power of enormous datasets to enable robust data management and fast, dependable access to information by employing partitioning and sharding strategies.

Stored Procedures and Functions

Stored procedures and user-defined functions are essential for database systems, providing powerful tools for encapsulating and reusing SQL code. These constructs enhance database operations' efficiency, maintainability, and security by allowing complex logic to be stored and executed on the database server rather than within the application code. Understanding how to create and use stored procedures and user-defined functions is crucial for optimizing database performance and simplifying application development.

Stored procedures are precompiled collections of SQL statements and optional control-flow logic stored under a name and processed as a unit. They are created to perform various tasks, such as data manipulation (INSERT, UPDATE, DELETE), data retrieval (SELECT), and complex business logic implementation. One of the critical benefits of stored procedures is their ability to reduce the amount of code sent from applications to the database, minimizing network traffic and improving performance. Because stored procedures are compiled and cached by the database engine, they execute more quickly than equivalent ad-hoc queries.

Creating a stored procedure involves using the CREATE PROCEDURE statement followed by the procedure's name and SQL code. For example, SQL CREATE PROCEDURE GetEmployeeDetails @EmployeeID INT AS BEGIN.

SELECT * FROM Employees WHERE EmployeeID = @EmployeeID, END.

This simple stored procedure retrieves details of an employee based on the provided EmployeeID. Once created, stored procedures can be executed using the EXECUTE or EXEC command, passing any required parameters.

User-defined functions (UDFs) are similar to stored procedures but differ primarily in their use and capabilities. UDFs can return a single scalar value, a table, or a complex data type and are often used to encapsulate reusable logic that can be applied within SQL statements. There are two main types of UDFs: scalar functions, which return a single value, and table-valued functions, which return a table.

A scalar UDF example might look like this: SQL.

CREATE FUNCTION CalculateTax(@Amount DECIMAL(10, 2))RETURNS DECIMAL(10, 2)AS BEGIN RETURN @Amount * 0.1,END.

This function calculates a 10% tax on a given amount. UDFs can be used in SQL statements just like built-in functions:

SQL SELECT EmployeeID, CalculateTax(Salary) AS Tax FROM Employees.

Table-valued functions are more complex and can return entire result sets, allowing for sophisticated querying capabilities.

Both stored procedures and UDFs contribute to better code organization and reuse. They enhance security by limiting direct access to underlying tables and encapsulating permissions within the procedure or function. They also provide a clear separation between the database and application logic, simplifying maintenance and updates.

In conclusion, stored procedures and user-defined functions are invaluable tools in database management, providing efficiency, security, and reusability. Mastering their creation and use is essential for developers and database administrators aiming to optimize database operations and streamline application development.

Advanced SQL Features

Common Table Expressions (CTEs), window functions, and recursive searches are advanced SQL features that expand the language's potential beyond simple data manipulation and querying. Without subqueries or self-joins, window functions allow computations to be done over a range of table rows connected to the current row. They can perform operations such as finding moving averages, rating rows according to specific standards, and calculating running totals within a window of rows determined by a partition or an ordering specification. By offering a clear and effective means of carrying out intricate computations directly within SQL statements, window functions improve analytical queries and lessen the requirement for substantial data manipulation in application code.

```sql
SELECT product, [2021] AS sales_2021, [2022] AS
sales_2022, [2023] AS sales_2023
FROM (

    SELECT product, YEAR(order_date) AS year, sales
    FROM sales_data

) AS source_data
PIVOT (
    SUM(sales)
    FOR year IN ([2021], [2022], [2023])

) AS pivoted_data;
```

Another valuable feature is that temporary result sets can be established inside the execution scope of a single SELECT, INSERT, UPDATE, DELETE, or CREATE VIEW statement, thanks to Common Table Expressions (CTEs). By enabling the creation of named temporary result sets that can be reused within a larger query, CTEs significantly enhance the readability and maintainability of queries. This functionality is particularly beneficial for enhancing SQL code organization, reducing redundancy, and breaking down complex queries into more manageable and understandable components. CTEs are often used in conjunction with recursive searches to tackle hierarchical data structure-related issues.

Recursive queries open up the possibility to query hierarchical data structures, where a record may be related to other entries in the same table, such as organizational charts or bills of materials. Recursive inquiries use a unique syntax (with RECURSIVE in PostgreSQL and SQLite, for example) to reference the result of a previous iteration within the same query, in contrast to typical SQL queries that work with flat data structures. Using an iterative technique, a single query execution can traverse hierarchical relationships and aggregate data from various levels of the hierarchy. Recursive searches are versatile and practical for parent-child connections, pathfinding, and hierarchical data processing.

When combined, window functions, CTEs, and recursive queries allow database administrators and developers to conduct complex data analysis and manipulation inside the database engine. By taking advantage of these capabilities, SQL queries improve expressiveness, efficiency, and maintainability, which lessens the requirement for intricate procedural code in application layers. Proficiency in these sophisticated SQL procedures is crucial for current database professionals who aim to optimize SQL's data management and analysis capabilities. It not only boosts productivity but also makes handling complex data scenarios easier.

Real-world Case Studies

Database management case studies from the real world demonstrate how database solutions are applied in various industries and how businesses use technology to solve complicated problems and increase operational effectiveness. For example, databases are essential to managing patient records, medical histories, and treatment plans in the healthcare industry. Healthcare practitioners use relational databases to guarantee patient data is safe, readily available, and compliant with legal requirements like HIPAA. This helps with accurate diagnosis, treatment coordination, and compliance. For instance, hospitals use robust database systems to combine information from several sources, allowing for more efficient administrative procedures and thorough patient care.

Database administration is essential for improving sales forecasting, inventory control, and customer relationship management (CRM) in the retail sector. Relational databases are used by retailers to monitor inventory levels, examine sales patterns, and tailor marketing efforts to individual customers. To ensure prompt replenishment and reduce stockouts, a retail chain, for example, might employ a centralized database to synchronize inventory data across numerous store locations. Retailers can also segment consumer data using CRM databases according to preferences and past purchases, which enables customized loyalty and incentive plans that improve customer happiness and retention.

Databases play a critical role in the management of transactions, risk mitigation, and financial institutions' regulatory compliance. Banks and investment firms process Millions of financial transactions daily using transactional databases to guarantee security and accuracy in money transfers, loan approvals, and account maintenance. Database technologies facilitate real-time analytics for regulatory reporting and fraud detection, allowing for prompt decision-making and compliance with strict compliance guidelines such as KYC (Know Your Customer) and Basel III. These solutions enable smooth client interactions across digital platforms and preserve confidence and security in financial processes.

Databases are crucial to the manufacturing industry's ability to schedule production, manage the supply chain, and improve quality control procedures. Manufacturers use databases to track finished goods and raw materials, keep an eye on inventory levels, and evaluate metrics related to manufacturing efficiency. To provide just-in-time inventory management and lower operating costs, an automotive company, for instance, would use a relational database to combine data from suppliers, production lines, and distribution networks. Databases for quality control assist in finding flaws and streamlining production procedures, guaranteeing the dependability of the product and client delight.

Databases are used by telecommunications businesses to handle massive volumes of subscriber data, service delivery, and network performance indicators. Telecom companies use relational databases to store call logs, billing data, and customer profiles. This allows for precise invoicing, customized service recommendations, and proactive customer care. With focused network improvements and infrastructure investments, telecom operators may improve service quality, forecast customer attrition, and maximize network capacity thanks to database-driven analytics. These features are necessary to satisfy the changing needs of digital connectivity and guarantee smooth communication for both companies and customers.

Real-world case studies illustrate the adaptability and power of database solutions in boosting customer satisfaction, decision-making, and operational efficiency in these and other industries. Organizations can get a competitive edge, manage risks, and adjust to evolving market conditions by implementing cutting-edge database technologies and utilizing insights derived from data. Successful database management system installations highlight the need for careful planning, a robust infrastructure, and constant communication between IT specialists and business stakeholders. Databases will continue to play a vital role as essential tools for organizing and interpreting data as industries change in the digital era. This will help to spur innovation and achieve sustainable growth.

CONCLUSION

"SQL for Beginners: Building Strong Database Foundations: Your Essential Guide to Querying and Managing Databases." This knowledge is not just theoretical, but practical, enabling you to navigate the world of relational databases with confidence. From building and modifying data structures to maximizing query performance and ensuring data integrity, you're now ready to apply these skills in real-world scenarios.

You have learned how to configure your SQL environment, comprehend and generate database schemas, run intricate queries, and handle transactions during the chapters. You have studied advanced subjects like indexing techniques, optimizing efficiency, and safeguarding databases, giving you a complete toolkit to address practical database issues.

Through the prepared examples and practical activities, you've gained valuable hands-on experience with SQL. This approach ensures that you not only understand the theoretical concepts but are also proficient in applying them in real situations. This practical understanding is a key asset in your journey to master SQL.

Proceed with your exploration and experimentation with SQL. The abilities you have gained here provide a solid basis for additional education and specialization. Whether your career goal is to work as a software developer, database administrator, or data analyst, the skills you have learned from this book will be invaluable.

We appreciate that you selected this guide to assist you in learning SQL. We wish you well in all of your database-related pursuits and urge you to keep strengthening the solid base you have already laid.

Thank you for buying and reading/ listening to our book. If you found this book useful/ helpful please take a few minutes and leave a review on the platform where you purchased our book. Your feedback matters greatly to us.